Computers,
Language Learning and
Language Teaching

NEW DIRECTIONS IN LANGUAGE TEACHING
Editors: Howard B. Altman and Peter Strevens

This important new series is for language teachers and others who:
– need to be informed about the key issues facing the language teaching profession today;
– want to understand the theoretical issues underlying current debates;
– wish to relate theory to classroom practice.

In this series:
Computers, Language Learning and Language Teaching by Khurshid Ahmad, Greville Corbett, Margaret Rogers and Roland Sussex
Beyond Methodology – Second Language Teaching and the Community by Mary Ashworth
Course Design – developing programs and materials for language learning by Fraida Dubin and Elite Olshtain
Developing Reading Skills – A practical guide to reading comprehension exercises by Françoise Grellet
Simulations in Language Teaching by Ken Jones
Communicative Language Teaching – An introduction by William Littlewood
Video in Language Teaching by Jack Lonergan

Computers, Language Learning and Language Teaching

*Khurshid Ahmad,
Greville Corbett,
Margaret Rogers and
Roland Sussex*

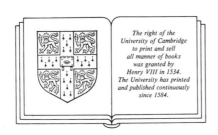

The right of the
University of Cambridge
to print and sell
all manner of books
was granted by
Henry VIII in 1534.
The University has printed
and published continuously
since 1584.

Cambridge University Press
Cambridge
London   New York   New Rochelle
Melbourne   Sydney

Published by the Press Syndicate of the University of Cambridge
The Pitt Building, Trumpington Street, Cambridge CB2 1RP
32 East 57th Street, New York, NY 10022, USA
10 Stamford Road, Oakleigh, Melbourne 3166, Australia

First published 1985

Printed in Great Britain
at the University Press, Cambridge

Library of Congress catalogue card number: 85–47549

British Library cataloguing in publication data

Computers, language learning and language
teaching. – (New directions in language teaching)
1. Language and languages – Computer assisted
instruction
I. Ahmad, Khurshid   II. Series 407'.8   P53

ISBN 0 521 26569 X   hard covers
ISBN 0 521 31957 9   paperback

Contents

143895

Preface

This book is an introduction to the use of computers in the teaching and learning of languages. It is intended for language teachers at all levels from primary to tertiary, including those in continuing education, and assumes no previous knowledge of computers or computing. Of the four authors, one is a computer scientist (Ahmad) and the other three are linguists as well as practising language teachers, with shared experience of using a variety of computers and of teaching several different languages. *Computers, Language Learning and Language Teaching* gives a survey of the field, judged against our own experience gained since 1976. It describes and analyses the role of the computer in language learning, and highlights the potential, the successes, and the pitfalls of this exciting new educational medium. The book is not written as a manual, but is designed to put CALL (Computer-Assisted Language Learning) in its historical and theoretical perspective, as well as drawing the reader's attention to certain practical conclusions.

We have learned a great deal from those who have worked with us over the years and gratefully acknowledge our debt to them, especially Mick Colenso, Janet Devey, Jean Edwards, Valerie Harmer, John Hodder, Anna-Maria Sabbione and Stephen Young. Our students, who so quickly find the flaws in our materials, have contributed in a fundamental way to our understanding of how computers can be used in language learning. We would like to express our thanks to our editor, Peter Donovan, for his enthusiastic and expert guidance, and to Judy Bridgeman, Amanda Butcher, Olga Keks, Pratana Phutrakul, Caroline Richardson and Carol Trumble for typing and word-processing the script, which was submitted to the Cambridge University Press in machine-readable form. Support from the UK National Development Programme for Computer Assisted Learning (Ahmad 1976) and the Australian Research Grants Scheme (Sussex 1983–5) is gratefully acknowledged.

The book is dedicated to all our colleagues in language teaching.

1 Introduction

In recent years the computer has established itself as an important feature of modern life. It is no longer a large, expensive machine used exclusively by specialists in major industrial corporations, government and the military. Many of us use computers daily, sometimes without even being aware of the fact. Banking, traffic control, word-processing, social security applications, accounting and record-keeping, design, office management, computer games, various hobbies – these are merely a few of the applications where computers are now a part of our everyday life. The computer revolution, as it is commonly known, is more than just a technological development. It may well change society as radically as did the Industrial Revolution.

The rapid spread of computers has been spurred by intensive development in the field of computer technology. Computers have decreased in price dramatically over the last ten years, and their cost continues to fall. At the same time they have become much more powerful, yet smaller in size, more adaptable, more flexible, and easier to use. As a result, schools and governments have devoted resources to 'computer literacy', or knowledge about computers and computing. This effort has benefited mainly the younger generation, while older people, unless they have had a particular professional reason to become involved with computers, have been much less affected. Many teachers fall into this category. This is one of the reasons why computers have been so slow to make a distinct mark on education. In societies which have already undergone great changes as a result of contact with computers, educational authorities continue to hesitate. The delay in utilizing the computer in teaching is not surprising when we consider the speed at which computer technology has evolved. Yet the computer is not so forbidding, and there is no doubt that it can make a useful contribution to teaching a wide spread of subjects, including languages, applying a very broad range of methodologies. Nonetheless, many teachers continue to show reluctance to approach the new technology, and this gives cause for concern.

Part of the difficulty lies in the way computers are presented to the teaching profession. There are few good introductions to the use of computers for educational purposes. Until quite recently there was little for the language teacher beyond a number of articles scattered through the educational and technical literature. Books on the subject have now started to appear, for example, Davies (1982), Kenning & Kenning (1983), Wyatt (1983a) and Higgins & Johns (1984); others are in preparation (for example, Last forthcoming a). There are in addition collections of papers (Hart 1981a; Wyatt 1983b). The aim of this book is to present the computer as an educational aid to the interested teacher. We shall cover those aspects of computers and computing which the language teacher needs in order to understand the use of the computer for teaching purposes. We shall describe the types of activity which the computer can handle, and the ways in which the teacher's accumulated experience relates to this new technology.

1.1   The role of the computer in learning

The computer is a tool, of itself incapable of action. It has no inborn wisdom, no mind of its own, no initiative, and no inherent ability to learn or teach. It will perform, with remarkable speed, exactly the instructions given to it by a human user. These instructions can be typed into the computer from a keyboard, or can be assembled in computer programs, which consist of series of instructions for the computer to execute. The computer is a servant. Its role in education is that of a medium. Far from threatening the teacher's position, it is totally dependent on the teacher in many ways: for example, it is unable to create educational materials without a human to direct it. All the linguistic material and instructions for its presentation must be specified by the teacher. It is the teacher, then, who can make the computer assume various roles.

This point is not always well understood, even in the literature on computer-related education. There is a whole host of acronyms which have grown up around the computer in education, and an equally large range of misconceptions about the precise role of the computer. Probably the most common term at the present time is 'CAI', for 'Computer-Assisted Instruction' or 'Computer-Aided Instruction'. The words 'assist' and 'aid' are significant. They point to the computer's subservient, auxiliary role. The word 'instruction' is also significant. It indicates a bias towards the teaching aspect. CAI is the usual acronym in the United States of America. In Britain the more recent 'CAL', or 'Computer-Assisted Learning', is more common and is now gaining ground in the United States in ESL circles. The name CAL focuses on the learning aspect of the process. In both cases the computer is an intermediary. At most, it is merely a part of the total learning experience.

While most of the common acronyms for computer roles in education start with 'C' and end with 'I' or 'L', the middle letter varies. The literature has 'CBI', for 'Computer-Based Instruction', 'CDI' for 'Computer-Directed Instruction', 'CMI' for 'Computer-Managed Instruction', and of course the parallel 'CBL', 'CDL' and 'CML'. CBI suggests that the computer has a more fundamental role in the education process than in CAI. CDI and CMI explicitly assign a more active and controlling role to the computer. Instead of merely presenting material and questions, and collecting and processing the student's responses, the computer actually takes decisions about the shape and structure of the material to be presented to the student. It checks the student's responses, the time taken through the session, and similar factors. On the basis of this information, it guides the student to different parts of the CALL program, to different CALL packages, or to other activities which do not require the computer, as preparation for the next computer-directed session. These decisions, however, are put into the computer by the teacher. Without such instructions the computer is powerless. It is the teacher who decides what degree of control the computer will have. The boundary between the 'assisted' and 'aided' types of computer-related instruction on the one hand, and the 'based', 'directed' or 'managed' types on the other hand, is not clear-cut. They represent differing degrees of control exercised by the computer on behalf of the teacher. For this reason we have called this book *Computers, Language Learning and Language Teaching*, with no explicit reference to assistance, aid, direction or management. The roles of the computer are varied and we shall use the most neutral term available, Computer-Assisted Language Learning, which is abbreviated as CALL (except when we refer to projects which use another term).

We start with the teacher, a class of students and a computer. The computer can be physically situated in the classroom. It may be in a special laboratory, perhaps as part of a language laboratory, or in a specially designated area of a library, or in any other convenient location where the student, or small groups of students, can work uninterrupted. The computer can even be located in the student's home. The teacher decides that a certain part of the curriculum can be handled on the computer. This 'part' might be anything from short lessons and exercises to a substantial section of a course. Alternatively, the teacher may wish to adopt the computer to develop certain learning skills. The computer can be used as the mainstay of a course, or for backup, revision, reinforcement, extension, or a variety of other purposes. It may communicate with the student visually by displaying text, graphics (diagrams, graphs, line drawings) or video images on a screen; it may also present sound, in the form of speech, music or other audio output, although there is to date no possibility of the user carrying on a spoken dialogue with the computer. The usual means of communication with the computer is by typing commands and responses at a keyboard.

This is the general nature of the computer as a resource at the teacher's disposal. What, then, are the positive elements which the computer can offer the teacher, and what are its disadvantages?

1.2 The advantages of the computer in language learning

It is helpful to divide the advantages of the computer into three types: those which are part of its inherent nature, those which benefit the teacher, and those which benefit the learner. We begin with the inherent advantages of the computer. It can, as we shall see, handle a much wider range of activities, and much more powerfully, than other technological aids. More than just this, the computer can offer interactive learning. This means that it can conduct a two-way learning session with the student. It is much more than a mere programmed textbook, whose powers of interaction are virtually limited to an ability to reveal the correct answer: the computer can 'assess' the student's response. It can also display messages, take the student through subsequent attempts at a question, and even take the student to a different section of the package, depending on the nature of the response. The computer can do all this very quickly – its response is practically instantaneous. If the computer is impersonal and literal-minded, it is also unfailingly accurate and precise. It does not tire, and its attention does not falter. It can repeat an activity with none of the errors which easily arise from repetition by humans, and it is as impartial and unbiased as the linguistic material which is typed into it. It can handle a very large volume of interaction and can deliver to the student feedback of some subtlety, at more frequent intervals than would be possible for a human teacher in all but individual tuition sessions. And it is flexible in a number of significant ways. It often happens that students cannot attend a class because of illness, timetable clashes, and other problems. This presents no difficulty for the computer. Provided a computer is available, the student can come at any time, and spend as long as is needed to gain full benefit from the material. It can accommodate different speeds of learning, or alternatively, limits can be imposed on the time available for answering questions, which is valuable when it is used for testing purposes.

From the point of view of the teacher, the computer presents several aspects of particular promise. Prominent among these is its versatility in handling different kinds of material. The simplest is the one-way presentation of information, in the form of text, graphics, audio and video. The computer can also handle question-and-answer routines, simulated 'dialogues', hypothesis testing, and many other types of exercise. It can choose questions in sequence or at random from the list of questions supplied by the teacher. It can 'branch' to different parts of the package, depending on many different factors, and can do so at any point. When the student has completed the session, the computer can record results, errors, success rates, the time spent, and much more information for the teacher to view at a later time. As a result of this information, or from the reactions of the students, the teacher is able to revise and refine the materials at any stage. Unlike a textbook lesson, which the teacher cannot change, and to which at best some subsidiary materials can be added, the computer exercise can be easily modified. This entire process does not even require the teacher to be in direct contact with the students – although we have found that CALL works best when integrated with normal classroom teaching patterns. The computer gives the student the opportunity to benefit from material carefully designed or selected by the teacher, without his or her actual presence. As we have said, this type of private practice facility differs from book exercises and language laboratories in that it is responsive to the individual student and is capable of assessing responses and acting accordingly, that is to say, it is interactive. All these factors have the effect of freeing the teacher from some constraints imposed by heavy teaching schedules. And this is particularly the case if the computer is handling drill and revision sessions, to which it is well suited. This will make more time available for creative and imaginative teaching in those parts of the course where teacher–student contact is more necessary.

For the student too, the computer offers many advantages. First among these is access. The computer's flexibility of time allows the student the choice of when to study particular topics and how long to spend on them. This factor makes many educational courses accessible to students who would otherwise have no chance to take them. More than this, the computer can also allow students to take courses, or parts of courses, at a distance. Distance teaching is eminently feasible by computer. Many computers can be linked by telephone lines or special land-lines, so that a student in, say, Australia could use CALL materials on a computer physically located in, say, Scotland (though the telephone bill would discourage this). Alternatively, teachers can send tapes or discs of their materials through the post. Whatever the factors of time and distance, the computer retains its potential for personalized instruction. The branching capacity which we have already mentioned means that the computer can be made sensitive to the learner's pace, pattern of responses, and so on, and can adjust the linguistic material to the needs of the individual. And the teacher, using the feedback and reports from the learner's performance, can tailor packages (linguistic data and programs) specifically to the needs of individual students with special learning problems. The learning session can also be more concentrated than normal class sessions. The student has the exclusive attention of the computer. There is no 'low attention' period as the student waits for his or her turn to come round in class. For all practical purposes, each student has the computer's full attention and can work at the speed best suited to the individual. Each student response receives a reply from the computer, virtually instantaneously, with appropriate feedback in the form of comments, assessment and guidance. Even the best teacher needs at least a day to mark and return students' work. The computer does the whole process at once. The learner is corrected the first time a mistake is made. The rest of the exercise, rather than perpetuating the error, can serve to practise the correct version. Such exercises are typically described as being in tutorial mode. While individual use of the computer is the commonest type of CALL, groups can also work at a single computer or terminal, in tutorial or non-tutorial mode. The computer may serve as an 'oracle': for example, if it has some part of the target language available for inspection (perhaps a set of sentences of a given type), the class can form hypotheses about regularities in the target language which can be immediately tested (and subsequently modified) using the computer. Or the computer can be used for simulations of various types, the aim of which is to stimulate group discussion on a specific theme in the foreign language.

Experience has also shown that learning with a computer is rated highly by students. There is the novelty of working with the computer, together with its diversity and sophistication. And there is the element of competition. Students like 'taking on the computer' and trying to beat it. Since many young people have in any case been introduced to computers precisely through games, they probably expect using a computer to be fun. Adapting and devising computer games for language-teaching purposes deserves more effort than has been devoted to it to date. Language programs might not match the success of Space Invaders, but there is no reason why learning a language should not be exciting and enjoyable.

Finally, the computer can be a powerful motivating force for productive study. CALL is still being evaluated; there are problems in assessing results – so much depends on course objectives, on what is tested and on the method of testing. Nevertheless there is evidence, which will be considered critically later, to suggest that drop-out rates are lower with classes using CALL; that achievement rates are at least as good as those of control groups not using CALL; that attention spans are longer; and that the material is usually better learnt, and learnt more quickly. For these reasons CALL deserves serious consideration.

1.3 The disadvantages of the computer in language learning

A mystique has arisen around the computer. Somewhere between fact and science fiction, the computer is often supposed to be about to take over many of the social and economic functions now performed by humans. We are offered visions of a world where all-powerful computers control the running of society, leaving human beings free to develop their creative talents – or to languish in eternal boredom, controlled by technology. Teachers are made redundant, and students learn everything from computers. Such forecasts are not feasible, at least in terms of computers and society as we now understand them. But they have been responsible for some of the prejudice against the introduction of computers in education. This prejudice constitutes a serious barrier to a proper understanding of the potential contribution of computers to areas like language learning, where the humanistic counter-reaction has been particularly severe. Typical examples are described by Olsen (1980), who conducted a survey of foreign-language departments at a number of American universities. He asked the question whether the department would introduce CAI by 1980. Some respondents made comments such as 'Forget it!' or 'Don't do it. It is a very stupid idea.' Some expressed the fear that CAI does not fit into the concept of a liberal arts college.

Prejudice aside, there are some genuine problems in using the computer for language teaching. Some of these stem from the nature of the computer itself, while others relate to the present state of CALL. The easiest way to start with CALL is to buy materials off-the-shelf or to borrow materials developed by colleagues. But computer programs are seldom 'portable'. Unless the computer is the same as the one on which the materials were produced, they will probably not run without modification. Such modifications may be prohibitively time-consuming, if not impossible. This situation is now being ameliorated with the appearance of more portable programs, but the underlying problem of portability is far from solved. And even if such CALL packages can be borrowed or bought, the quality of a lot of CALL material leaves much to be desired. Like any other educational materials, CALL programs need to be evaluated. So even for those teachers who do not wish to develop their own CALL programs, a knowledge of their operation and possible scope is essential for assessing their potential value.

There is, in addition, the question of the range of activities to which the computer can contribute. While the computer is able to accommodate a substantial range of learning styles, it is certainly not a complete substitute for a teacher. The material which can usefully be handled by a computer represents at best a tiny fraction of the linguistic knowledge which a teacher brings to bear in a language class. What computers can do is present text to the student, and given the right equipment, provide graphics, video and audio. But the majority of computers can accept from the student only responses typed in via the keyboard or, with special equipment, made by touching the screen or indicating a position on it using the so-called 'mouse'. In question-and-answer learning, the variety of responses which a question can evoke from the student must therefore be carefully anticipated by the CALL author. The computer, in short, cannot effectively conduct an 'open-ended' dialogue with the student. It has neither the vocabulary, nor the ability, to understand the enormous range of utterances possible in any human language. It cannot handle ambiguity with any confidence. It can 'learn' only in a restricted sense (though this question is currently the object of intensive research under the heading of 'fifth generation computers'). All this means that the computer can be used only for certain types of teaching, and only with certain types of material if used in a tutorial mode. However, language teachers must be prepared to explore ways of using the computer so as to take advantage of its special capacities. The computer is an excellent medium for simulations (changing the conditions on the rules of inflexion, word-formation and syntax, for example). It can also be used to generate language, including words and word-forms, phrases and sentences. These uses, however, require substantial preparation and skilful programming.

The development of CALL programs requires knowledge of three fields: competence in the target subject area, pedagogical skill, and computing expertise. In language teaching it is seldom the case that any one individual is sufficiently versed in all these skills from the beginning. There have been various attempted solutions to this problem.

One solution is for computing and language experts to work together. An advantage of this approach is that a relatively high level of sophistication may be offered on both sides. Given the long preparation time (some authors spend several hundred hours producing packages that students will use for an hour), it is sensible to work in a team when possible. Against this there is, ironically, the problem of communication: each side must understand what is significant or problematic for the other. It is important that such points be made explicit, since otherwise the eventual form of the CALL package may be distorted.

For the teacher who wishes, or who is forced, to go it alone in the development of CALL programs, there is always the possibility of learning a programming language. It has been estimated that a language such as BASIC could be learnt in a fairly short time, counted in days rather than weeks. Davies (1980:6) has claimed that 'compared with French and German, BASIC is a doddle'. This approach has two major advantages. The first is that learning a programming language is in itself a worthwhile step for a language teacher, particularly for the insights it gives into the structure of natural language. The second is that the teacher is not forced to write programs in any particular mould. It should be said that BASIC, though widely available, is not ideal for CALL purposes. More advanced languages such as PASCAL, SNOBOL, LISP and PROLOG have attractions for language teachers. (Programming-language names will be given in capitals, whether or not they are acronyms.) However, it takes a considerable time for the teacher to gain sufficient mastery of any programming language to do what he or she wants with it. In the initial stages, progress is likely to be slow, and the form of the teaching materials produced may well be determined more by what the teacher can program than by pedagogical considerations.

A third alternative is provided by author languages, which enable teachers to produce CALL materials more quickly and easily than would be possible with an ordinary programming language. The teacher has available a limited set of easily understood commands. These commands are translated into a programming language, and the teacher devising the program need not be concerned with computing procedures. The features available vary from one author language to another. Author languages offer the opportunity to write successful programs with less effort than that required to master a conventional programming language. A disadvantage is that they also exclude certain possibilities and so tend to discourage innovative work.

A final alternative for those who wish to develop their own programs involves so-called authoring packages. These are working routines, already programmed, into which the teacher simply inserts the relevant data or corpus required for the exercise. This is done by having the teacher respond to requests for information, which the computer displays on the terminal in ordinary language. The teacher types in the instructions which the learner will have to follow, the exercise task – examples with gaps for instance – and the expected answers. Other features may also be built in: whether the user should have a score and the number of attempts at the answer to be allowed. Authoring packages allow the teacher to write programs with minimal computing knowledge. They are therefore an easy way to begin. However, the package necessarily restricts the form of what the teacher can produce even more than do author languages. Authoring packages are usually confined to the question-answer type of exercise and are generally linear, with no branching facilities.

We must not forget the practical matter of equipment. Particularly in secondary schools, computers have been used mainly for scientific subjects and, to a lesser extent, for subjects like economics and geography. Language teachers often do not try to use the computer and, when they do, there may be incredulous (and defensive) colleagues who are suspicious of new users for equipment which may already be heavily used. Beyond this, there is also the whole question of learning to use a new technology, and one which may not be easily accessible, particularly for teachers in the humanities. In order to make productive and creative use of CALL, the teacher must come to grips with the computer, and must understand the ways in which it can relate to language teaching, and to a particular class. And while it is not necessary to become a computer programmer, it is still necessary to come quite some distance to meet the computer on its own ground. One of our motivations for writing this book was precisely the lack of a suitable introduction to guide teachers along this rewarding path.

1.4 Towards a synthesis

The preceding two sections show the computer's potential and its disadvantages. We aim to show how the teacher can exploit the computer's potential, while overcoming and adapting to its disadvantages.

This book is intended for language teachers and all those interested in language and its relation to the computer. The book is descriptive rather than practical. It surveys a range of aspects of the computer in language teaching, and draws on many different examples, but it does not aim to be a practical introduction to writing CALL packages. We assume no previous knowledge of computers or computing. In chapter 2, therefore, we introduce some basic concepts of computing. (Teachers already involved in computing may wish to omit this chapter.) Chapter 3 is concerned with the development and history of CALL, and traces the emergence of some of the dominant themes in CALL practice and research today. Chapter 4 investigates in more detail the relations between the learner, the computer and natural language, and the implications for the teacher wishing to use CALL. In chapter 5 we give a concrete example of a CALL program in tutorial mode, considering some of the questions which are of relevance for evaluation. Chapter 6 takes the teacher some distance into the question of programming languages, and outlines some of the types of conceptual framework which the teacher must master in order to create viable and educationally interesting CALL materials. In chapter 7 we consider the total range of CALL and the computer, and define the areas in which the computer has a role to play, as well as those areas where current technology falls short of the requirements of language teaching. And in chapter 8 we describe some of the areas which are under development, and where, given the breathtaking pace of advances in computer technology, we can expect some substantial progress in the next few years.

If the language-teaching profession does not begin to pay serious and considered attention to computers, it may well get left behind as others take advantage of this powerful new resource. We do not believe for a moment that the computer will take over language teaching. It is not a self-sufficient means of language teaching, but rather a valuable aid which should take its place alongside other already established devices for helping the language learner. Nor does its use presuppose any particular approach to language teaching. But we maintain, on the basis of experience with CALL and a knowledge of the dynamic growth of CAL in general, that computers have much to offer to language teachers and language learners. Our aim is to describe CALL, its nature and its operation, so that those engaged in teaching and learning languages can appreciate how they may use, and how they might contribute to, this promising new development.

2 Hardware and software

Hardware is the name given to computers and the various pieces of equipment attached to them. Hardware is hard in the sense that we can see it and physically touch it: the keyboard, the screen, the cabinets containing the computer itself, and any peripheral machinery like printers and disc drives are all hardware. By analogy, the term **software** is used to describe the less physically tangible programs that control the computer, and the material which the computer presents to the student. In a certain sense software can be seen, when it is printed out on paper (hard copy), but unlike the hardware proper, software is essentially a set of instructions to the computer, and so is 'softer' – less physically concrete – than the machines themselves.

2.1 Hardware

In this section we shall consider hardware from the point of view of the CALL teacher. This is not the place for a general introduction to computers. There are now dozens of books about computers and computing for the beginner which describe computers and how they work. The language teacher needs to have only a limited knowledge about computers in order to become competent in CALL, and we shall concentrate on those parts of computers and their operation which are relevant to language teaching.

2.1.1 Computers

Most people nowadays have at least a rough idea of what a computer looks like: a keyboard similar to that of a typewriter, a television-like screen, and various boxes, which fit easily onto an ordinary desk. This picture, however, is true only of the microcomputer, which has made extraordinary strides since the mid 1970s. As recently as the 1960s a computer filled several large rooms. Yet these early machines could not compete in speed or capacity with many small modern computers. Computers have not only shrunk in size; they are also now very much cheaper than they were, and some experts estimate that their cost has gone down more than a thousand-fold in the last decade. All this means that the computer is now physically and economically within the scope of the home enthusiast. It also means that computers are well within the budget of many educational institutions.

Modern computers, of course, are not all of the small, desk-top variety. Large computers, which are used in some specialized applications in meteorology and physics, speech recognition, machine translation, and certain military areas, still occupy whole rooms. These computers are called **mainframes**; middle-sized computers are called **minicomputers**; and the smaller computers are known as **microcomputers**, or simply **micros**. They all have the same basic components: a **Central Processing Unit (CPU)**, which performs all the calculations and directs the operation of the other components of the computer; and devices for getting information into the computer, storing it there, and getting it out again. In general, the larger the memory, the more powerful the computer. Computer memory is usually measured in kilobytes, abbreviated as 'K' or 'Kb'. A **kilobyte** is 1024 bytes. The **byte**, in turn, equals eight bits. A **bit**, or *bi*nary digi*t*, is the smallest unit: it can be thought of as a simple choice between a '1' and a '0' (section 6.1.1 gives more details). A set of eight bits (a byte) is sufficient for storing any one of the characters on the keyboard: a letter, a digit or one of the other signs. The computer manipulates several bits simultaneously in a group called a **computer word**. A computer word may consist of eight bits (in which case a word equals one byte) or it may equal, say, sixteen or thirty-two bits. The larger the word size, the more powerful the computer. It is important to note that a computer word is very different from a word in natural language. To store a natural-language word typically requires several computer words.

Memory capacity is important for CALL use on micros, where each user has his or her own computer. A reasonable size of machine to start on CALL would be 32K. Memory capacity is not so relevant for larger computers, which in some cases can allow over 100 simultaneous users, and work by **time-sharing**, that is, allowing each user in turn a small fraction of time each second. Unlike some engineering and scientific applications, CALL does not make heavy time demands on computers, and many users can work at the same time without overloading the system. Modern computers work at phenomenal speeds: they can perform an addition in the time it takes light to travel a foot; and some computers can perform about 10 million addition operations in a second.

The CALL teacher need not know a great deal about the computer's internal workings; the computer is a 'black box' which does what it is told, in a very fast, but also very literal-minded way. What concerns the CALL teacher most is getting linguistic material into the computer; instructing the computer how to present the material to the student; and how to keep track of or respond to the student's performance during the CALL sessions. This information, and these instructions, can be changed by the programmer or the CALL teacher.

2.1.2 Terminals

The computer is powerless unless the teacher can put programs and associated linguistic material (i.e. data) into it and get information out of it. For these purposes a **terminal** is required. We will consider terminals which are used with mainframes (and minicomputers) first, since here the notion is more straightforward. To put material into the computer, the user normally types at a typewriter-like keyboard connected to the computer. The typing and the computer's responses are displayed on a screen, which resembles a television screen. The keyboard and screen together are known as a **visual display unit** (**VDU**). The VDU is a particular type of computer terminal. The terminal can be physically remote from the computer, being connected to it via a land-line, similar to a telephone line.

A visual display unit

Initially, CALL sessions were conducted on a different kind of terminal, called a **teletype** – a specialized typewriter/printer which prints on paper.

Teletypes have even been adapted to handle alphabets ('character sets') other than English, but they are slow and noisy in comparison with the VDU, which is silent and has the potential to accommodate specialized character sets, pictures, diagrams, graphs and colour (though these depend on the particular VDU). Unlike the teletype, a VDU does not provide a permanent record of a session; if one is required it is necessary to use a printer (see section 2.1.4).

For CALL purposes, the teletype has been superseded by the combination of keyboard and screen, the VDU. Microcomputers also normally use a keyboard and screen. However, rather than being physically remote, they may be part of the computer itself. The keyboard may be housed in the same case as the computer proper (CPU and associated input and output units, see section 6.1.2). Microcomputers may use an ordinary television set as the display screen; alternatively a special-purpose screen can be used. This is called a **monitor**. When purchasing equipment it is important to ensure that the monitor is fully compatible with the microcomputer.

A typical microcomputer with keyboard

Whether a microcomputer or a mainframe is involved, the basic devices for input and output – a keyboard and some type of screen – remain the same. The keyboard has a number of special keys to convey specialized instructions to the computer – operations like deleting a line of text, or sending a command. The layout of individual keyboards differs in some details, though the arrangement of letters usually follows the QWERTY... pattern. Some keyboards, especially on microcomputers, are also able to reproduce sound as either music or speech – though the quality of such sound reproduction is often not very good (section 8.4). It is more common to find only a facility to produce 'beeps', usually programmed to warn the user that an error has occurred. Just as on a mainframe terminal, the monitor displays what the user types at the keyboard. It also displays the computer's responses, and the results of the computer's operations and calculations on the data entered by the user. These messages and information can be in the form of words or sentences in normal language, in mathematical or other special notation, or in graphs, diagrams and pictures. The monitor may display in white on black, green on black (phosphor-green monitor), creamy brown on dark brown, or it may be a full-colour monitor.

The same equipment is used both by the teacher to set up CALL programs, and by the student to run them when finished. CALL activities may require other peripheral equipment (for example, to give sound output). The combination of the terminal and any additional equipment is called a **work-station**.

2.1.3 Memory and storage

As we saw in section 2.1.1, computers are more or less powerful, generally according to the size of their memory. The nature of the computer memory is also important to the CALL teacher. There are two broad categories of computer memory, that which the computer requires for its own operation, and that which is available for running the particular user's programs. Each time the computer is switched off, the latter type of memory is wiped clean. If the keyboard were the only means of getting data into the computer, the teacher would have to type in the CALL materials each time the computer was switched on. The computer's answer is to provide a means of **peripheral storage** for such material – peripheral in the sense that it is physically separate from the computer's main memory. It can be used for the permanent storage of data, and can be called into use at any time.

There are four main means of peripheral storage available at the present time: cassette, magnetic tape, floppy disc and hard disc. When these are connected to the computer, it obtains data from them in a similar way to that in which it takes input from the keyboard. The cassette and magnetic tape use the same type of magnetic tape as a cassette-recorder; many small computer systems use a standard cassette-recorder to store data and programs.

Microcomputer with cassette-recorder and monitor

Although a cassette is the slowest way of storing and retrieving information for the computer, it is certainly the cheapest. In contrast, computer
tape proper is wider than the tape used in normal reel-to-reel tape-
recorders, and is commonly used for storing large quantities of information. Such tapes can store 1600 'bits' of information per inch, so that a
tape 2400 feet long can store 46 million bits of information. Magnetic
tape is reliable and fairly cheap, but it takes a relatively long time to search
the tape for a given piece of text or information. The machines which are
used to read and write such tapes (tape drives) are expensive, which
explains why they are not usually found on microcomputers.

Discs are much faster than tape. They are called **random access** storage
devices, because the computer can look for information anywhere on the
disc without having to check from start to finish. These discs rotate at high
speed below a record/read head which can deposit or retrieve data very
quickly. Even with the slowest disc, data can usually be located in less
than one-tenth of a second, and can be read into the computer's memory
at rates approaching 3000 bytes per second. These figures apply to floppy
discs, which are flexible (hence 'floppy') discs about the size of a 45 rpm
gramophone record. Hard discs are much faster, and can hold much
larger volumes of information. Hard discs, which used to be available
only on larger machines, are now being increasingly used for microcomputers. Floppy discs, however, are still the standard disc for micros.

One of the reasons for their popularity is price: a disc can cost as little as $3 or so, and can store from approximately 100,000 bytes to well over a million bytes. Furthermore, floppy disc drives are relatively inexpensive.

On a large computer installation, all the physical tape and disc operations are carried out by technical staff, and the teacher will quite likely never set eyes on either the tapes or the discs. Microcomputers are provided with detailed instructions for using both tape and disc, and present no significant difficulties. If the CALL materials are on disc or tape, all the teacher has to do is to instruct the computer, by typing in the necessary instructions at the keyboard – to read the appropriate programs and data into its memory after loading the disc or tape. The CALL materials are then ready for use.

2.1.4 Printers

Electronic storage media like tapes and discs are fast and permanent, but they can only be read through the computer. The teacher may require a permanent record of certain CALL materials or of a particular CALL session. In some cases it may be useful for the student to have printed records of a session as well. To do this a printer is required.

Microcomputer with printer and floppy disc drives

A normal electric or electronic typewriter can be used as a printer, i.e. an output device, provided that it is equipped with a suitable interface, which converts the computer's output into signals which the typewriter/printer can 'understand'. There are also special-purpose computer printers. Some of them operate with 'daisy-wheels' or 'golf-balls', which can handle foreign alphabets if given the right instructions from the computer, and if the appropriate printing element is available for the language required. Other printers can print patterns of dots to form not only letters but also diagrams, graphs and pictures ('dot-matrix' printers). The printer can produce a copy of any text or portion of text in the computer, irrespective of what is currently displayed on the screen. Some printers can also copy the contents of the screen itself, including any combination of letters and pictures which it is currently displaying. In general, only the daisy-wheel or golf-ball printers will deliver letter-quality results, though some dot-matrix printers are now getting closer to this goal, and the laser printers now coming on the market are able to produce print-quality output at astonishing speeds. On the other hand, a dot-matrix printer can deliver perfectly legible – if slightly 'spotty' – results, which are quite adequate for most CALL purposes.

2.1.5 Hardware configuration

There are three principal configurations of computer systems: the **stand-alone** system, the **multi-user** system, and the **networked** system. The stand-alone system, as its name implies, is a self-contained computer. The CALL teacher will meet the stand-alone system mainly in the form of the microcomputer, which caters for one student (or group working together) at a time. The multi-user system, sometimes with more than 100 simultaneous users, requires a minicomputer or a mainframe.

The computer shares out its time to each user in turn. The **time-sharing** mechanism allocates each user a fraction of each second, and if the user's instructions cannot be completed in that time, it returns to complete the job on the next cycle of time-sharing. CALL is an ideal activity for computers which can support multiple users since it does not require a great deal of computing power, and machines can support a large number of CALL users simultaneously without being forced to run unrealistically slowly. As mentioned above, the terminals can be located near the computer, or they may be connected to the computer by a special direct line (a land-line), or even by a normal telephone line. If the prospective CALL teacher's institution has such a computer, the easiest way to introduce CALL is to attach suitable terminals to the existing computer. This means that students at various different locations can use the CALL materials, an important factor when some of them may have difficulty in attending all the normal classes with the teacher.

A minicomputer

Computers can also be **networked,** that is, physically separate computers and terminals can communicate with each other. This facility is
potentially important to the CALL teacher, since it means that the stand-
alone units can be linked into a single network rather than functioning as
discrete units. One of the computers may act as a manager of the network,
and the rest of the computers acquire information from it, and pass

information to it, through a system of connexions like a telephone exchange. The control which the teacher can exercise over such networks (or, for that matter, in CALL operations running off a single minicomputer or mainframe) allows smooth running of CALL material. It is also possible to link into large external networks and so take advantage of materials already developed elsewhere. Well-known networks of this type are EDUNET in the United States and PLATO's UNIVERSE.

A larger computer installation showing disc drives in the foreground

2.2 Software and courseware

The word **software** was created by analogy to hardware. Software refers to the **programs**, or sets of commands, by which the computer is instructed to perform specific tasks. The computer can be programmed to carry out tasks like reading or storing data, analysing data, performing logical and arithmetic operations, and reporting back to the user. Within the area of software, a distinction between general purpose computer programs and and teaching materials has grown up and the term **courseware** is sometimes used for CALL (or CAL) materials and any associated documentation for use by students.

2.2.1 Software

The role of computer programs in CALL has caused many misunderstandings, and has certainly not contributed to the spread of CALL through our education systems. Programming languages like BASIC and PASCAL are often regarded as difficult to learn, particularly by teachers in the humanities. Teachers considering the use of CALL sometimes get no further than this problem, since they suspect that regardless of whether they have the gift and the inclination to handle programming, they do not have sufficient spare time. However, there are ways of introducing and implementing CALL which require no programming at all by the teacher. Alternatively, those who want to develop CALL materials themselves can learn to write simple but effective programs for the computer in a surprisingly short time.

There are many programming languages. By human standards these are poor languages, with a vocabulary of 100 words or less, and simple and rigid syntax. But they allow no ambiguity, and so can tell the computer exactly what the user wants it to do (see section 6.3). Among the more widely used programming languages are BASIC, FORTRAN, PASCAL, COBOL, C, LISP, SNOBOL and PROLOG. Only BASIC and PASCAL are widely available on microcomputers as well as on larger machines. BASIC is easier to learn and use; PASCAL is more powerful. Learning to write simple programs in either language is not as difficult or abstruse a business as it is sometimes supposed to be, though it takes time and experience before the CALL teacher will be able to produce CALL materials which are really interesting from the educational point of view.

A CALL program may display text, information, prompts and questions, pictures, graphs, game formats, and so on to the student. It can determine whether the student's responses are right/wrong or appropriate/inappropriate, and then present the student with the next question, phase of the game, and so on. It can keep score, and display the score (or not, as the teacher may determine). It can record scores, errors, and a host of other information for the teacher to examine, in order to find out how well the students are progressing and how well the CALL materials themselves are performing. This is only a small sample of the range of interactions which the computer can handle in the context of CALL. Given a program which runs successfully, it may be possible to use it as a **template** to develop further materials. In other words, the structure of the program is left untouched but the linguistic material is changed. To take a simple example, if a vocabulary-testing program is available, a second program can be developed by retaining the essentials of the first program but adding a different set of vocabulary items. From the student's point of view, the amount of material has been doubled; however, the effort involved in producing the second program is a fraction of that required to write the original program. Here is part of a simple BASIC program to show how easy it is to alter the material:

```
100   PRINT   "Welcome to Lesson 4."
110   PRINT   "If you would like to revise some vocabulary, press V."
120   PRINT   "If you would like to take the comprehension test"
130   PRINT   "immediately, press C."
140   INPUT   Q$
150   END
```

This program will display on the screen:

Welcome to Lesson 4.
If you would like to revise some vocabulary, press V.
If you would like to take the comprehension test
immediately, press C.
?

The question mark indicates that the computer is waiting for a response from the student – in this case, what the computer knows as "Q$". If the teacher wants to make a small change, for example from 'Lesson 4' to 'Lesson 5', a change in line 100 in the program is all that is required:

```
100   PRINT   "Welcome to Lesson 5."
```

The rest of the program can then be re-used in its original form. The alteration to line 100 is a trivial matter. This can be carried out using a program called an **editor**. This makes it easy to change material or to insert new material. It is part of the software normally supplied with the computer, and so the commands are specific to particular machines.

There is a slightly different approach in which the software which runs the CALL session and the linguistic material are more rigorously separated. The program which handles the display of material, checking responses and so on, is then termed the **driver program**. The actual material to be displayed, the questions and answers, comments and explanations, in fact all the linguistic data, are stored separately in a **lesson file**. In computing terms, a **file** is a quantity of related data normally stored in peripheral memory, for example, on disc or cassette, and read into the main memory when required.

It is possible to separate the driver program from the lesson files using a programming language such as BASIC (for details see Kenning & Kenning 1983:93–114). However, special **author languages** make this separation easier for the teacher. They allow the lesson files to take the form almost of ordinary text, with just a small number of special labels to be interpreted by the driver program. Here is a simple example from the E/MU author language (developed at the University of Melbourne). It covers the same text as in our previous example of BASIC. But it is closer to ordinary English, and so is easier to alter if the teacher wants to use it as a template:

```
.TEXT.
Welcome to Lesson 4.
If you would like to revise some vocabulary, press V.
If you would like to take the comprehension test
immediately, press C.
?
```

Note that there are no line numbers; and there is no risk of omitting the command PRINT or the vital inverted commas required in the BASIC program. The label '.TEXT.' instructs the driver program to display on the screen the material which follows it. In the E/MU system the labels have a line on their own, and begin and end with a full stop (period). This much has to obey strict conventions. But the rest of the text can be altered to suit any message in the target language or the learner's first language.

Writing such material is not difficult. Once the teacher has worked out the subject matter of the CALL package and has the text, questions and answers ready for presentation, it is only a matter of interspersing the appropriate author-language elements. The labels and conventions of the author language are kept as limited and as transparent as possible, and the transition from ordinary lesson material to CALL material is a relatively straightforward one. This approach bypasses the difficulties of learning a programming language.

There are other ways to make life even easier for the teacher beginning with CALL. The teacher can be provided not only with all the components which we have already described, but also an **authoring package**. In essence the authoring package (sometimes called an **authoring system**) takes the teacher through the process of writing a lesson, giving prompts at every step by means of a 'menu', or a list of actions which the teacher can take: for instance, display a page of text, ask a question, specify a right answer, and so on. In such lessons the teacher does not even have to learn the author language, but 'talks' to the computer through the authoring package, and in something approaching natural language. The authoring package accepts the teacher's linguistic data and inserts the necessary author-language commands for future use by the driver program.

To date, an authoring package is the easiest way to construct CALL programs; using an already existing program as a template is slightly less easy. Probably next easiest is writing lessons using a simple author language. On the other hand, it is harder to write CALL materials directly in a programming language like BASIC. But the point to be made here is that – as our example suggests – BASIC is not too difficult to master. Certainly, knowledge of a programming language offers the fullest range of possibilities.

This is all that we shall say directly about software here, though the question of writing a CALL program will be taken up in more detail in chapters 5 and 6. However, as we have seen, the teacher does not need to become directly involved in the software itself unless he or she so wishes; a general notion of its purpose and function will suffice. This is clearly the case when the teacher purchases the CALL materials, although this background knowledge is of course useful when evaluating them.

2.2.2 Courseware

As mentioned above, **courseware** can be used to refer to software specifically designed for teaching purposes. The term may also cover any associated materials which the student uses while working with the computer. It is also worth noting here the terms 'CALL program' and 'CALL package'. They are often used interchangeably in the literature. Strictly speaking, a **package** is a suite of programs and associated linguistic data, which go together to form one piece of courseware. From the learner's point of view, the distinction is irrevelant. Courseware is a particularly appropriate term when materials are purchased ready for use. Off-the-shelf courseware is the teacher's easiest introduction to CALL. If courseware is available (see 'Useful addresses') which meets all the technical and educational requirements of the teacher, then using it will save an enormous amount of time. Assessing courseware for suitability, however, is not an easy matter.

In the first place, there are technical questions. The teacher must make sure that the CALL package will actually run on the equipment available. CALL courseware is often not **portable**, i.e. cannot be run on more than one make of computer. Making alterations to computer materials can be a very expensive process. In some cases it is virtually impossible to adapt a given piece of software or courseware to run on certain computers. Unless the CALL program can be demonstrated in operation on a computer identical to the computer which the teacher will use, then there will almost certainly be problems in getting it to run, and some of these problems may turn out to be extremely time-consuming, if not insoluble.

There are also many questions of educational content and design which the teacher must weigh up. The best way to start is to get some expert independent advice from a language teacher who is already either using the CALL package under consideration, or who has experience of CALL. Teachers' resource centres, which are increasing in number, can be an excellent place to find advice and materials. Although CALL materials are being developed at numerous locations around the world, the package in which the teacher is interested may not be available in an accessible place. Moreover, it is not always possible to see courseware being demonstrated by someone both knowledgeable and objective. However, publishers' demonstrations and language-teaching conferences can provide good opportunities to see what is available.

Documentation for CALL packages is often not complete, or not pitched at the right level, particularly for the teacher who is working his or her way into CALL. And assessing CALL materials at a distance is a very difficult task, since the teacher is entirely at the mercy of existing descriptions of the package, which may or may not be unbiased. There are so far no generally accepted criteria or guidelines for assessing CALL packages, and teachers should treat with some scepticism any unsubstantiated claims about courseware from commercial or non-commercial sources. In chapter 5 we examine a particular CALL program, suggesting points to be borne in mind when evaluating such materials.

2.3 Conclusion

Hardware and software are both vast subjects in their own right. However, the teacher can work with only an elementary knowledge of each. It is certainly helpful to know the main characteristics and capabilities of the hardware available. Similarly, it is also useful to be familiar with the most common terms used to describe software. The teacher can choose between a range of options from purchasing off-the-shelf materials to developing packages in a programming language, according to interest or time available. It is not essential to learn a programming language but, as we shall see in chapter 6, knowledge of a programming language can be an advantage to the language teacher.

3 The development and background of CALL

CALL, as we have seen in chapter 1, arose from the combination of two separate factors: educational needs and technological means. But CALL, like CAL in general, did not simply emerge ready-made from the direct application of the computer to teaching and learning; it has evolved over a period of time. Developments in CALL can be traced back to the 1960s: the PLATO project, a large system developed at the University of Illinois, and the computer-based foreign-language-teaching project at Stanford University, led the way in the evolution of CALL. Both were developed on large computers. At the other end of the size scale, there has been a flurry of largely unrelated activity in CALL over the last few years, prompted by the emergence of inexpensive microcomputer systems. These trends have common historical roots. Although the computer's educational potential was being discussed as far back as the late 1940s, it took some time for educators to begin to assess the educational nature of the computer, and the ways in which it could be adapted to, and integrated into, learning programmes and curricula. It is impossible to appreciate the nature and significance of modern CALL without an understanding of its evolution, of the progressive realization of the computer's potential for linguistic purposes, and of the ways in which the computer has combined with other resources to create a viable learning environment.

Modern CALL is the result of the convergence of several lines of research into the use of computers in handling language. Some of this work has been directly concerned with language teaching, and the history of this component of CALL shows how computers and programming have been combined for specific teaching purposes (section 3.1). But there are three other lines of research which have had an important influence on the evolution of CALL, and of ideas about the working relationship between computers and language: experiments in programmed instruction (section 3.2), developments in computational linguistics (section 3.3) and work on machine translation (section 3.4). Experiments with programmed instruction have had a direct bearing on CALL. Developments in computational linguistics and machine translation had an indirect but important influence on CALL, since research efforts in the two fields clearly determine the 'limits' of computer usage in literary and linguistic research and so by implication also define the 'limits' of computer usage in language teaching and learning. Computational linguistics and machine translation are of importance to CALL for two reasons: first, those working in these areas have provided some of the tools for CALL, such as particular features of programming languages; second, they form part of the groundwork for future developments, as they will lead to more intelligent processing of grammar and meaning and therefore to more sensible responses from the computer.

3.1 CAL in language teaching: a short history (1965 onwards)

The late 1960s and early 1970s are of particular historical importance for CALL. The rapid development in computer technology, together with the use of computers by linguists and literary researchers, paved the way for the introduction of computers in language teaching and learning. Reviews of work in CALL during the decade 1963–73 are given by Allen (1972, 1973a) and Roberts (1973); there are also two annotated bibliographies, one covering the period up to 1973 (Allen 1973b) and the other for the period up to 1977 (Birdsong 1977). More recent bibliographical work is referred to in the introductory note to our bibliography. For a general picture of the use of computers in education at the end of 1960s, not just in language teaching, the reader should consult the collection of papers edited by Atkinson & Wilson (1969) and for a recent critical overview O'Shea & Self (1983:67–126). We shall consider work specifically related to language teaching in the United States and Great Britain. Recall that CAI, Computer-Assisted Instruction, is a term used widely in North America, whereas CAL, Computer-Assisted Learning, is the usual term in Britain. In the United States, we assess the work of teams at Stanford University (section 3.1.1), at Illinois (section 3.1.2), and at Dartmouth (section 3.1.3). The review of work in Britain concentrates on that of Alford (section 3.1.4).

It will become apparent that easy access to computer systems has contributed much to the growing use of computer material in language teaching. Institutions which had access to time-sharing systems and sophisticated terminals (in some cases including touch-sensitive screens, foreign alphabet input/output, audio output and so on) still use CALL material. It is equally important to note that CALL during the decade 1965–75 was almost entirely geared towards teaching the written language and towards beginning students.

3.1.1 The Stanford project

The work in foreign-language teaching at Stanford dates from the mid 1960s. Most of this work was carried out under the supervision of Van

Campen in the Slavic Languages Department. An important point about Van Campen's early work, a computer-based introductory Russian course, was that it was self-instructional: most of the teaching material was on the computer. The exercises were similar to those of a conventional introductory Russian course, but the material was presented in a programmed format. The students were asked to type answers to questions stated in Russian, to inflect words, and to perform various types of transformation exercise. Remedial branching programs (section 4.4.3) were also included and a progress report on the student was kept by the computer.

The equipment consisted of a teletype which could be used to input/output in Roman or Cyrillic scripts. The teletype was co-ordinated with a tape-recorder, which was used only to ask questions. It was not possible for the student to answer questions orally. The equipment was supervised by postgraduate students, who assisted in case of difficulties with the teletypes, and in some cases with the Russian also. The students on the Stanford Russian course also participated in traditional language-laboratory exercises. Twice a week the students made recordings, which were then evaluated by their teachers. The results of the Stanford introductory Russian course by computer were promising. Those students who used the computer-based material scored significantly better than those who who were taught conventionally. Van Campen believes that: 'the introduction of computer-based instruction in *elementary* language courses in which the *acquisition of writing* plays an important role would greatly improve the effectiveness of those courses' (1968:27, our emphasis).

Van Campen's introductory Russian course was the basis of further computer-based courses in Old Church Slavonic (Van Campen 1973), Bulgarian (Karriker 1976), the History of the Russian Literary Language (Schupbach 1973), and more recently initial Armenian (Van Campen, Markosian & Seropian 1980). A significant amount of material was developed for these different languages: the Russian course lasts for 170 hours, while the Bulgarian, Old Church Slavonic and the History of the Russian Literary Language courses each last for forty hours. The 170-hour Russian course could be scheduled by the student over an academic year. Self-pacing and ease of availability certainly contributed to the success of the Stanford program. While work at Stanford was first made available in report form, the most accessible source of information is Suppes (1981). The work done at Stanford on the reading curriculum is also of interest (Atkinson 1968 and references there).

During the course of the project, the hardware at Stanford has changed significantly. Instead of the slow teletype there is now a bilingual visual display unit, and in place of the tape-recorder there is a computer-generated audio system. This audio system is used to store and reproduce

29

sound according to the instructions within the program (see section 8.4 for more details).

3.1.2 The PLATO system

Another successful project in computer-based education is the Programmed Logic for Automated Teaching Operations (PLATO) system. The PLATO system was developed at the University of Illinois, in conjunction with the Control Data Corporation, with a view to servicing the needs of computer-based education across the range of disciplines taught at a conventional university. The PLATO system consists of computers and terminals manufactured by the Control Data Corporation together with the special purpose software to develop CAL material. These materials can only be run on PLATO (CDC) hardware. One measure of the success of the PLATO system is its ability to survive (and thrive) over a period of two decades and to sustain the interest of teachers.

Curtin *et al.* (1972) were among the first teachers to use the PLATO system for language teaching. The aim of Curtin's group was 'to teach students to translate written Russian into English', especially those students 'whose needs are most effectively met by teaching the decoding of the written language directly' (1972:354). Curtin *et al.* further argue that since a computer-based system 'calls for high frequency of student response to visual devices, the student's full attention is concentrated on the lesson. Through the use of the computer the student is taught to translate Russian prose with a minimum expenditure of his time' (1972:354). Grammar is presented as an aid to translation and the interactive environment expedites the whole learning process. Curtin's Russian reading course consists of three major components: (a) vocabulary drill, (b) brief grammar explanations and drills, and (c) translation tests at various intervals, concluded by a final translation test, which measures the student's comprehension of written Russian. The course is divided into sixteen units and takes around seventy hours to complete. Usually after every third or fourth lesson there is a translation test reviewing the student's progress, and depending upon the marks scored in the tests, the student is automatically given remedial work where appropriate (Curtin, Cooper & Provenzano 1981).

Common sense and the assorted disaster stories of the machine translation experiments probably motivated Curtin to include the 'Sentence Judger' option in her course. She remarks that the variety of possible translations of a Russian sentence makes a straight comparison of the student response with one English sentence unworkable. The Sentence Judger program performs three important functions: (a) it looks for key-words or synonyms in the student's answer, (b) it indicates misspelling, and (c) it allows the prescription of word order. For example, the correct translation of *Istoriyu pomnit Amerika* is 'America remembers history'. The Sentence Judger will reject answers like 'History remembers America', which could arise if the student failed to recognize the accusative ending of *Istoriyu*.

Curtin's Russian course involves an interesting blend of two types of computer program: those which conduct vocabulary drills and give explanations, mark the student's replies and monitor student progress and so on; and the 'word-processing' type of programs. The latter programs were used exclusively by the teachers to format and layout the text which the drill programs output. The value of this facility is illustrated by the following quotation: 'when the student explores verb conjugations, each new verb appears as a series of automatic displays in which the ending of the verb varies with the pronoun used. By underlining the pronoun and the ending of the verb as the changes occur, we focus the student's attention on the importance of endings to convey meaning' (1972:356). Curtin's course utilized bilingual terminals capable of inputting/outputting in Roman and Cyrillic: even as far back as 1972, when the norm was to display text in only one alphabet, the PLATO system needed no transliteration: text could be displayed in many different alphabets, all on the same screen.

During the 1970s the PLATO system made considerable progress. The range of languages covered is extensive: there are publications referring to the teaching of languages including Chinese, English, Esperanto, French, German, Hindi, Latin, Modern Hebrew, Modern Greek, Norwegian, Russian and Swedish. The insistence is still, very pragmatically, on drill and practice. However, the exercises include tackling phonemic and graphemic problems in Hindi, logographic problems in Chinese and playing the game 'Hangman' in Modern Hebrew. The PLATO system 'talks' to the student: it can give dictation, for instance. More importantly the motivation behind the production of PLATO langage materials has been practical; the aim was not 'to investigate abstract theories of lesson and curriculum design' (Hart 1981b:12). For a full account of the use of PLATO for language teaching, the reader should refer to Hart (1981a) and Chapelle & Jamieson (1983).

The PLATO system has managed to keep up with the state of the art in computer technology. During the middle to late 1960s, when it was normal to use teletypes (working at 10 characters per second), the PLATO system featured an interactive facility, accessed by VDUs (working at 30–120 characters per second). In the early 1970s, when sophisticated graphical and text display was essentially the domain of the high-technologists, the PLATO system terminals allowed language teachers to generate sophisticated graphics and to display text in a variety of non-Roman scripts. Nowadays, when most student input to the computer system is still via a keyboard, the PLATO system offers touch-sensitive screens. This means that if the screen displays: 'Is your answer YES or NO?', all the student does to indicate an affirmative answer is to touch the word YES on the screen. This removes the possibility of typing mistakes – an important consideration for beginners and less dexterous users. The programming aids on PLATO include an author language called TUTOR, which not only allows the teacher to produce a tutorial drill or other type of exercise, but also helps to format and layout the text to be displayed, as mentioned above. The teacher can highlight, underline and paginate the text, box specific items, and so on. However, while PLATO offers a high degree of technological sophistication, it is also extremely expensive.

3.1.3   Work at Dartmouth

Dartmouth College, in New Hampshire, was also among the first academic institutions to provide a time-sharing (or interactive) facility to its user community in the late 1960s. The speed of response made possible by the time-sharing facility meant that the system could interact with the user. Today we tend to take interactive working with a computer for granted. But it should be remembered that, until quite recently, the normal way of working with a computer was in **batch mode**: data and programs were input, usually on punch cards and other paper media, while output (normally paper-based) was collected at a later time, quite often not even the same day.

Among the other 'firsts' the Dartmouth system provided was the BASIC programming language (Beginners All Purpose Symbolic Instruction Code), specifically developed for the novice programmer. It is easy to use and has good facilities for handling textual data. Language teachers started to use the Dartmouth time-sharing system in 1970 (Waite 1970). The languages covered were Danish, French, German, Latin and Spanish (Roberts 1973). This was later extended to include, among others, English and Russian (Scherr & Robinson 1980).

Waite developed 'two series of programs to assist students enrolled in elementary Latin courses' (1970:313–14). Drills included filling in blanks in a sentence, selecting the item which does not belong to a group, and selecting the best of four translations of a Latin sentence into English or vice versa. There were also vocabulary drills based on an introductory Latin textbook where the student was expected to give the Latin word corresponding to a series of English meanings, to give an English meaning for a Latin word, and to supply principal parts and meanings of Latin verbs. The student also had an option to ask for the answer directly by typing the question mark symbol on the keyboard.

Allen, also at Dartmouth, developed teaching programs for French and Danish to supplement regular classes. He notes that 'there is a direct relationship between a student's ability in a language and the proportion of time he spends with a computer and that it is possible to decrease the amount of time spent in class and still progress at a normal rate, if students supplement their work with well designed programs on a computer' (1972:48).

The programs developed at Dartmouth pay special attention to the automatic handling of minor typing errors in student answers. A simple program was developed to remove punctuation and extraneous characters, to make the letter 'l' equivalent to the number 1, and to remove extra spaces. Allen also describes more complicated programs which check for other typing errors and help to concentrate the students' attention on the quiz (question–answer routine) rather than having them struggle with the keyboard. The randomization of the questions asked by the program is also an important aspect of the work done at Dartmouth. Allen argues that the presentation and repetition of material in a predetermined sequence (as found in programmed instruction, see section 3.2) probably lead the student to establish a 'correct' order of answers by running the program several times. Randomization, on the other hand, prevents the student from simply retaining the correct answers as an associative chain. The availability of computing resources (with time-shared hardware and easy-to-use software) must have certainly motivated the program authors at Dartmouth to pay detailed attention to the requirements of the student.

Developments in computer-based learning in English include an interesting set of programs for teaching composition. These programs are aimed at beginners and were developed at the Department of English (Bien, private communication). Bien produced a set of eight programs, which include topics like the use of the apostrophe in possessives and in certain special plurals, the use of the colon and semicolon, and punctuation of independent and dependent clauses. The programs are self-documenting: when a particular program is run, it can also print a paper copy of the outline of the subject matter covered and explain specific points in varying degrees of depth.

3.1.4 The Scientific Language Project (University of Essex, 1965–9)

The Scientific Language Project, led by Alford, was designed to provide computer assistance in reading specialist texts in Russian. The major beneficiaries of the project were researchers and academics in science and engineering. Alford found that with computer assistance 'any individual can read material of his own choice at an acceptable speed after about 25 hours of initial study' (1971:5).

Alford argued that the computer provides assistance by supplementing the limited vocabulary of the initial learner. This is achieved by using the computer essentially as a memory device. It can store thousands of words and associated meanings; it can also be used as a clerical aid for presenting data in 'numerous ways which increase the efficiency of memorization' (see also section 8.1). The system worked as follows. A scientist, typically with a rudimentary knowledge of Russian but with a need to understand a particular research paper, was given two computer print-outs. In the first print-out, the entire text was reproduced in a single vertical column and against every word an appropriate dictionary entry was given. In the second, the vocabulary of the text was produced in frequency order with a dictionary entry against each word.

In this project the learner, the computer and aspects of language teaching were considered in a coherent fashion. Alford seems to have been influenced by the work in machine translation and computational linguistics, and was aware of the limitations of the technology and of the linguistic theory available during the late 1960s. His report sets out clearly the problems associated with reading foreign-language texts, discusses the solutions available and finally outlines the implementation of the project.

Alford's main concern was that, although by 1965 10 per cent of younger British scientists had completed a Russian course with very high rates of success in learning grammar, it still took the scientist 'about eight hours to read an average 3,000-word paper' (1971:7). Constant use of the dictionary was distracting and vocabulary learning was extremely slow. Alford's learning strategy takes into account the vocabulary-related statistical data, which show that for a given text containing a quarter of a million words, a small number of high-frequency words will cover a significant proportion of the text: 50 words will cover 34 per cent of the text, 100 words will cover 45 per cent of the text and 2750 words will cover about 96 per cent of a given specialized text. Alford argued that the person who can recognize the 1000 most common words in a particular subject will, on average, meet only one or two new words per sentence. But, when 3000 high-frequency words are known, only about one word in a paragraph presents a problem. Alford stressed that: 'Apart from two or three dozen grammatical words, 80–90% of HF [high-frequency] words are lexical items which vary greatly even between the specializations in one subject' (1971:11).

Alford favoured context-free learning of vocabulary as a first step because it can be selective. Once the student has learnt a number of high-frequency words in a context-free manner then, when faced with a text: 'The advantages of contextual learning are increased by the degree of reading fluency which comes from the knowledge of a high percentage of text words' (1971:14).

A number of programs were written to set up and update dictionaries, and for look-up and data-display purposes. Alford's system as a whole was labour-intensive, which was inevitable given the computer resources of the time. Each research paper had to be transcribed into the computer by using slow teletypes. In addition, profitable reading of a particular paper depended on the availability of a specialist dictionary already stored on the computer system. Alford's arguments for the use of computer resources indicate that he was clear about what computers can and, more importantly, cannot do. His work has recently served as the basis for a course run by Siemens at their Educational Centre in Munich to help German electrical engineers read reports in English.

3.1.5 The microcomputer boom

The examples we have used so far in relation to the development of CALL typically use mainframe computers. Developments in computer technology meant that some of the mainframe capabilities became available on microcomputer systems. The late 1970s will be remembered as a period in which the microcomputer established itself as a consumer product. Microcomputer sales are now quoted in millions; retailers of various types stock 'micros' as well as the programs accompanying the machines. The programs are categorized as recreational, commercial and educational. The educational programs almost invariably include some language-teaching programs. The relative cheapness of the microcomputer means that computing facilities are now much more widely available. The teacher may well have access to a machine at work or at home, and it is probable that several students in a given class will own one. Microcomputers offer certain advantages over mainframes since they are normally used on an individual basis: the microcomputer is not remote either in the physical or the psychological sense of the word. The microcomputer user need not worry about gaining access to the computer system, for example. Nash & Ball (1982) and Smith (1982) describe the possibilities offered by the microcomputer for CAL in general. Of course, microcomputers are less powerful than mainframes, but their capabilities are impressive. Michael Carr, Roy Bivon and Jeremy Fox (University of East Anglia) have shown that micros can support a range of CALL programs. These programs include a student monitoring system (section 7.3) and an authoring package (section 6.6). They use the Apple-II with two disc drives. Tim Johns (University of Birmingham) has devised a range of text-based programs, which run on smaller micros (Johns 1982). A recent collection of articles on the teaching of English as mother tongue and as a foreign language describes several imaginative possibilities for expanding the range of CALL activities using the microcomputer (Chandler 1983).

   While interesting work is being done on microcomputers, there is nevertheless a profusion of trivial and boring packages. Partly to blame are the limitations of microcomputers in terms of the available programming languages and other programming aids, as well as the hardware, particularly the limited storage capacity. In addition, many authors are unaware of previous work done in CALL. This means that mistakes made on mainframes are being repeated, and accumulated wisdom is being ignored. Indeed, Howe & du Boulay (1979) are concerned that for CAL in general, microcomputers are turning the clock back. It is, perhaps, not surprising that the microcomputer boom has as yet done little to advance the standard of CALL programs. The real contribution of micro-computers has been to extend *access* to computers enormously. With so many more language teachers using computers, we must hope that some will have the imaginative ideas which will lead to a new generation of more sophisticated CALL packages without the errors and omissions of the previous generation.

3.2 Programmed instruction

Many CALL programs exhibit features which are reminiscent of pro-grammed instruction, a popular pedagogical development, principally in the United States, during the 1950s and 1960s. Programmed instruction was based on behaviourist theories of learning, which have since been seriously questioned. The theoretical basis of programmed instruction was provided by Skinner, who claimed that: 'Special techniques have been designed to arrange what are called "contingencies of reinforcement" – the relations which prevail between behavior on the one hand and the consequences of that behavior on the other – with the result that a much more effective control of behavior has been achieved' (1954:86). Skin-ner's work on teaching what he calls 'very complex *sequences* of sche-dules' (1954:89) via behaviour modification with pigeons and a large number of vertebrates (including rats, dogs, monkeys, human children and psychotic patients), led him to believe that: 'In spite of great phy-logenetic differences, all these organisms show amazingly similar pro-perties of the learning process' (1954:89). Reinforcement of 'correct behavior' played an important part in Skinner's model of learning. He was, however, one of the first, within this limited model, to point out in a formal manner the importance of feedback.

A student taught by programmed-instruction techniques was presented with a sequence of teaching frames which, by gradual steps, built up the behaviour to be acquired. The student's participation was ensured by requiring an active response to each frame. The programmed-instruction practitioners stressed three principles: minimal steps, individual learning pace and immediate reinforcement. Minimal steps were provided by specially prepared textbooks and tapes. Individual learning pace was catered for by giving the students easy access to the books and tapes and other materials (Clark & Clark 1966; Mueller & Niedzielski 1966; and references in Ornstein 1968). And immediate reinforcement was provided either by textbooks containing the correct answer or by chemically sensitive paper. The latter required a special pen: a number of possible answers to a question was offered, each answer being placed in a box. If the student wrote in the correct answer, the colour of the paper changed. In addition, various proficiency tests were administered at given intervals. Interestingly, Skinner estimates that to bring about 'efficient mathematical behavior', somewhere between 25,000 and 50,000 contingencies are required for a given pupil (1954:91–2). Yet the rules of arithmetic are quite straightforward, and the symbols involved are well adapted to machines. If we extend the argument, relating this number of contingencies to the complexity of rules in natural language, then this gives some indication of the enormity of the problem facing the language teacher. The practitioners of programmed instruction in language teaching, however, took the business of 'behavior modification' seriously: for example, the teaching of pronunciation became the shaping of 'pronunciation behavior' (Mueller & Niedzielski 1966:92).

Studies of the programmed-instruction projects indicated an important advantage of such techniques: since correction, however it was implemented, was impersonal, a failure to respond correctly did not cause the learner the embarrassment which is typical in some student–teacher interaction (see also a critical survey of projects in the United States by Ornstein 1968). Reports of students' progress using programmed instruction (Meyer 1960; Clark & Clark 1966; Prince & Casey 1972) show higher scores in proficiency tests, and good grades with a minimum expenditure of time (but Clark & Clark wonder whether the students who opted for programmed instruction were well motivated in the first place and thus worked better). Another interesting observation concerned drop-out rates. Mueller (1968:81) reports that in a conventionally taught French course the drop-out rates were 30 per cent and 40 per cent in the first two years (rates considered to be 'normal'). The drop-out rate for students taught on programmed-instruction courses was 15 per cent and 12 per cent. It also becomes apparent that the later protagonists of programmed instruction place particular stress on the role of self instruction rather than the 'teacher-less' aspect of such language classes (Porter 1960:187). Teachers are, in fact, regarded as an important part of the whole set-up: 'The instructor's role is changed. He still motivates the students, corrects and helps, but no longer drills' (Ornstein 1968:80). Although critical of programmed instruction, Ornstein notes that programmed instruction was used over a range of languages, from French, German, Russian and Spanish, to Arabic, Thai, Vietnamese, Mandarin Chinese, Ukrainian and Haitian Creole.

Perhaps because of the development of the subject, perhaps because of the criticism, the later programmed-instruction practitioners stressed that as far as language learning is concerned they do not operate within the 'narrow Skinnerian concepts with operant conditioning as its principal feature' (Mueller 1972:148). So new phrases like 'Designed Learning' or 'Compensating Instruction' were introduced.

Fragmentation of the subject matter, a central behaviourist feature of programmed instruction, was noted by many authors including Pressey, the inventor of the modern teaching machine. Littlewood has addressed this problem in some detail. He argues that 'in analysing language and language skills, we think in terms of discrete items; in actual language activity, however, this large number of skills, units and systems is closely integrated' (Littlewood 1974a:14). He goes on to ask the important question whether once the lesson has been presented in fragments, the teaching programme can 'enable the student to reintegrate them into structures'. Littlewood quotes an example of a lesson unit which teaches that French intervocalic /z/ is spelt 's', and points out that 'this fragmentation quickly destroys essential elements of language to the point of making it unrecognizable'.

A survey of the literature on programmed instruction in the language field shows that the discussion of pros and cons was rather heated. Hocking notes that some teachers rejected the use of any machines including teaching machines and the language laboratory. He quotes a defiant school teacher as saying 'I don't advocate the use of machines . . . Give me a small class and plenty of resources. Let the lab be for 1984 and Big Brother . . . God preserve us from the machine!' (1970:79). Further on, Hocking quotes a wag who comments that 'academic Luddites flaunt their innocence of electronic equipment – even television – like a badge of honour or a warrant of electronic virginity'.

A much more well-founded objection arose from developments in thinking on the nature of language learning which rejected Skinner's behaviouristic model with its roots in animal behaviour. The impetus to this fundamental change came from the work of Noam Chomsky, in particular his review (1959) of Skinner's *Verbal Behavior*. The debate over the advantages and the disadvantages of programmed instruction, especially in the context of language learning, continued over two decades (roughly 1954–74). From that debate the following points emerge as being of particular relevance to CALL:

(a) Programmed instruction laid great emphasis on breaking the learning task down in a highly directive way into small discrete steps. A similar approach was found in much early work in CALL, and is still in evidence today.

(b) Programmed instruction can be applied to the more specific, less elusive areas of language (Ornstein 1968). The most obvious areas are morphology, vocabulary and certain parts of syntax; these have been taken up in many CALL programs.

(c) Most aspects of language taken in isolation could in principle be presented in a programmed-instruction format. It is in the process of integration for communication purposes that the problems arise (Littlewood 1974a:15). The question of integration for communicative purposes remains problematic for CALL.

(d) The presentation of specific formal areas of language in discrete steps provided a context in which students could determine their own pace of learning. Self-pacing is an advantageous feature of CALL; however, self-pacing is equally possible with lesson models which are very different from those found in programmed instruction.

(e) Provision of immediate feedback to the student was an essential part of the programmed-instruction approach to learning. It is also widely quoted as a positive feature of CALL, since the computer provides feedback on written work much more quickly than the teacher can. The major advantage of CALL over programmed instruction in terms of feedback is in its ability to give much more finely tuned information (based on the student's current or previous answers or on the computer's own representation of the subject area).

The legacy of programmed instruction in CALL is in some ways an uncomfortable one. On the other hand, CALL can in certain respects take over and improve on the positive aspects of programmed instruction. Many of the issues touched on in this section are dealt with in more detail in chapters 4 and 7.

3.3 Computational linguistics

CALL is not the only area where computers and natural language meet. Two very important developments which arise mainly out of the use of computers in the context of natural languages are computational linguistics and natural-language processing.

Computers have been used as a research tool in linguistic and literary research for over two decades. Wisbey (1962) pioneered the 'art' of concordance-making by electronic computers while analysing a German literary corpus. The annual bibliographies of relevant journals (for example, *Computers and the Humanities*) bear witness to the middle-to-late 1960s growth in the use of computers as a research tool in a variety of subjects under the general umbrella of literary and linguistic research. Projects included stylistic and content analysis, authorship attribution studies, lexical studies, and analysis of certain aspects of syntax, to name but a few. See Bott (1970) for a readable exposition of computational linguistics. An interesting account of work in the Soviet Union is given by Knowles (1982).

Computers can be used to scan large quantities of textual material (corpora) of interest to a linguistic or literary researcher, and to collate data related to selected items, for example, the total number of occurrences of a particular adjective in a given corpus. The collated data are then processed by the computer according to a set of instructions given by the researcher to the machine. The researcher can produce various index arrangements of the extracted data. Howard-Hill (1979:3) defines two important index arrangements, the verbal index and the concordance, as follows: the verbal index is an alphabetical list of the words in a text corpus, and refers to those parts of the text corpus where the individual occurrences of the word may be found; the concordance differs essentially from the verbal index only in that the use of each item is shown in its context by a quotation drawn from the text.

Initially, computational linguistics was used largely in the pursuit of traditional objectives such as creating concordances, which could be achieved more effectively by using a computer. However, developments in the theory of grammar, in particular the work of Chomsky, radically influenced computational linguistics. Chomsky's rules of syntax have the necessary mathematical and logical apparatus to motivate people familiar with computers to implement these rules on a computer system, in other words, to 'model' aspects of natural language on a computer.

Work in natural-language processing, or making the computer 'understand' natural-language input, is still in its early stages. It comes under the umbrella of artificial intelligence (section 8.3). Some of the difficulties posed by natural language for the computer are discussed in section 4.2. Of course, the way in which the computer 'understands' natural language may be very different from the processing strategies adopted by humans. Nevertheless, this is an area where the work of linguists and that of computer scientists are complementing each other.

Developments in this area are of vital importance to CALL. Pusack(1983:63) has remarked that 'truly effective foreign-language CAI must be sought in approaches which automate grammatical systems in the answer-processing step'. An interesting application of parsing theory for CALL purposes is reported in Markosian & Ager(1983). The understanding of natural language on the part of the computer will contribute to the fluency of the interaction between the human user and the machine, which uses natural language as a medium. There is indeed enormous commercial and military interest in systems which can understand natural language. It is a highly desirable feature of any interactive computer system, not only those intended for educational purposes, that the machine should understand the language input by the user. Of course, in CALL the problem is multiplied by the fact that the subject matter, not only the operational dialogue, is concerned with natural language.

3.4 Machine translation

The concept of machine translation has been attributed to the ancient Greeks, who 'talked frequently about the ideal language which could replace existing languages after being subjected to mechanical treatment' (Zarechnak 1979:12). Machine translation, or attempts at translating written text from one language to another using a machine, have approximately followed the development of computers and their early variants, calculators. Zarechnak (1979:7) names two early inventors in the field of 'mechanical translation': the Frenchman Georges Artsruni and P. P. Trojanskij from the USSR, who had invented machines for translating natural languages as long ago as 1933. Artsruni even had a patent for what was referred to as a 'Mechanical Brain'.

Trojanskij's mechanical machine consisted of a tape moving across a table on which words or units from various languages were written in vertical columns (one-to-one equivalence). Trojanskij, according to Zarechnak, divided the automatic translation process into three stages. The first is analysis, which transforms the input text into a particular logical form; all the inflected words are represented in canonical forms – nouns are represented in the nominative case, verbs in the infinitive and so on. The second stage is transfer: with the help of a machine-readable canonical dictionary and the transformed text, the 'transfer' takes place without any human intervention. Then follows synthesis, which performs the analysis stage in reverse for the target language: the raw translated words are converted into the required grammatical forms. Trojanskij's machine could only be used in the transfer stage of translation, but he was convinced that the whole translation process could be automated (Zarechnak 1979:8).

The destruction wrought by the 1939–45 war reinforced the ideal that people of the world should be able to communicate better, for instance, by reading research or newspaper reports published in a foreign language. Some members of the post-war scientific community thought that machine translation could be implemented in the near future. Particularly influential were Weaver and Booth. Weaver's famous memorandum (1949), which contained 'some comments and suggestions bearing on the possibility of contributing at least something to the solution of the world-wide translation problem through the use of electronic computers of great capacity, flexibility and speed' (1949:15) was an impetus to much of the early work.

Their imagination had been fired by the 'stored-program' computer and advances in the interdisciplinary field of cryptographic analysis. The 'stored-program' computer not only stored abstract concepts like numbers and text strings (textual material), but was also able to store a sequence of instructions, and to manipulate the numbers and the text rapidly and consistently: this is what we know as the computer program (section 6.1.2 gives more details of the 'stored-program' computer). The matter then was very simple: if you have a mass of text in a foreign language stored on a computer, all that is needed is a dictionary in the target language and a sequence of instructions to replace each word of the foreign language with a corresponding word in the target language. This rather simple-minded approach to natural language is a source of many, now stale jokes, such as: 'What did the computer reply when asked to translate "out of sight, out of mind" from English to Russian and back into English?' Answer: 'Invisible idiot'. Indeed, as philosophers like Russell and Quine had already stated, it is the sentence and not the word which is the minimum carrier of meaning. Languages are not differentiated simply through their lexical systems, but also through their syntactic and semantic structure. As Winograd pointed out (1973:152), translation 'could not be treated as a problem of rearranging syntactic structures and words, because attention to meaning was required even to achieve moderately acceptable results'.

Progress in machine translation was hampered by two major problems: a lack of sophistication in computer technology and a different, but equally limiting lack of sophistication in linguistics. Computers in the 1950s and 1960s were not advanced enough to deal with natural language; they were cumbersome and very slow machines. The programming languages available were probably suited to solving the complex equations of mathematical physics, but were hopelessly inadequate for various linguistic operations. Equally, the state of linguistic knowledge was certainly overestimated by the machine translation experts of the post-war era. The simple 'mechanical' task of dictionary look-up was found to be too onerous at times, and even then inadequate; sometimes translation requires real-world knowledge which goes well beyond that found in dictionaries (Bar-Hillel 1960:158–61). It was also apparent that traditional grammars are of little use in the machine translation environment. Problems in the areas of morphology and syntax were to wait for a decade for breakthroughs in computational and theoretical linguistics. The elusive areas of semantics and knowledge representation are still areas of intense research and development. Indeed, the early exponents of machine translation like Dostert appreciated that '1. linguistic problems were too difficult for any practical experiments, and 2. experiments were the only way in which the subject could make progress at all' (Zarechnak 1979:14).

Machine translation is becoming increasingly important in a world which relies heavily on the written word and where it is becoming harder to match for every language pair required with human translators. For every new country which joins the European Community, the number of language pairs increases dramatically. If the number of languages increases from nine to ten, the number of translation pairs increases from thirty-six to forty-five. At present the SYSTRAN system, based on specific language pairs, is used for translation in particular subject areas. The Community has proposed an ambitious machine-translation system called Eurotra (King 1982). In the United States (MacDonald 1979) and in the USSR (Zarechnak 1979) work is continuing on translation systems which are already in operation. There are now several commercially available machine-translation programs (both for mainframes and for microcomputers) with prices ranging from $10,000 to over $100,000. Some of these programs produce so-called 'high-quality' translations, which in some cases can translate scientific documents with an accuracy of 80 to 90 per cent. However, pre-editing of input and/or post-editing of text output has come to play an essential role (Lawson 1982).

Current research effort in machine translation is concentrated on developing more sophisticated syntactic and semantic representations of natural language which could be implemented on a machine. This is obviously of relevance to CALL. There is also considerable activity generated in the field of machine translation by work initiated by the Japanese on Fifth Generation computer systems. One essential part of the Japanese programme is a machine-translation system capable of working with an accuracy of 90 per cent; the cost of such systems must be 30 per cent or less than that of human translators (Moto-oka *et al.* 1982:38). Current efforts point towards the need for an 'expert system': a suite of computer programs which enables human beings to represent and subsequently apply human knowledge of various forms. In the context of operational machine-translation systems, these knowledge forms include 'syntactic, conceptual and common sense' (Whitelock 1983:19).

3.5 Conclusion

As we have seen, the development and background of CALL are complex. Major projects like those at Stanford, Illinois and Dartmouth form the mainstream of development; it appears that the availability of intelligent terminals (capable of handling foreign-language scripts, sound and graphics) and non-numeric programming languages made a significant contribution to the success of these projects. Alford's work showed how the computer can be used as a resource which may be tailored to the specialist needs of particular users. But broader issues concerned with the relation between the computer and natural language mean that CALL continues to find an important stimulus in work on computational linguistics and machine translation. It is important to note that some of the projects we have discussed were very ambitious (machine translation), and some were pragmatic (CALL work at Stanford, Illinois and so on) in the sense that the linguists and language teachers involved had a clear notion of the limits of computers. They perceived that language is a complex whole, and that the theoretical framework to describe it, even in parts, is still developing.

It should by now be clear that there is a considerable body of experience relevant to CALL, some specifically in teaching projects and some in related disciplines. In certain areas of both hardware and software we have facilities which the pioneers could only dream of. Yet there is still a great deal to be learned from their work.

4 The learner, language and the computer

Our attention has so far focused mainly on computers (chapter 2) and on the relationship between computers and natural language as in, for instance, computational linguistics and machine translation (sections 3.3 and 3.4). In CALL there is of course a third element: the learner.

In this chapter we consider the relationship between the learner and the computer (section 4.1), then we expand on the relationship between the computer and natural language (section 4.2), and thirdly, we discuss the question of the learner and natural language (section 4.3). We conclude with a discussion of some of the ways in which these three aspects of CALL can be approached in practice. In figure 1 we give a simple model of how these elements interact.

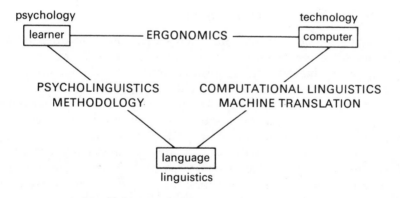

Figure 1 A model of the three main factors in CALL (learner, language, computer)

Future developments in CALL must be based on adequate models of the three corners of this triangle (learner, language, computer) *and* on the relationships between them. So far, we know a considerable amount about the way computers work. We know much less about natural language and even less about the process of language learning. The gaps are therefore for theoretical linguists and psycholinguists to fill by building models which can serve as a basis for more 'intelligent' computer programs (see section 8.3 on artificial intelligence).

4.1 The learner and the computer

We begin with ergonomics, the most concrete of the three relationships. The science of **ergonomics**, or 'human factors engineering', describes the relationship between people and machines. It relates to the design of machines, machine systems and work methods, and aims to optimize the productiveness of human users while also taking into account their comfort and safety. There are two ways in which we can consider the relevance of ergonomics to CALL. The first is the physical environment, the physical and mental comfort and convenience of the learner when operating the program. The second concerns the design of the program in relation to the user's needs. Both these factors are important, although they are distinct issues from the pedagogical and programming considerations which are usually regarded as central to CALL. However, without a comfortable physical environment and a 'robust' program, CALL will not work effectively.

4.1.1 The physical environment

Some of the physical considerations may seem nothing more than obvious common sense, but their importance needs to be stressed. The first consideration is the location of the microcomputer/s or the mainframe terminal/s (see section 2.1.2). They should not be put in a room where there is a lot of noise. Students should also have easy access to the machines if they are to be used outside normal classroom hours. In other words, machines should not be located in a distant annex, and the booking system should be as straightforward and accommodating as possible. Access to tapes, discs and printed material must be easy and reliable. Lack of organization in this respect can be annoying if students arrive to find the equipment already occupied or the discs unavailable.

Apparently simple issues are important for the success of CALL. For example, there must be adequate room for students to put books and writing materials next to the terminal. Another feature which will encourage continuing use of CALL is the use of disc drives as opposed to cassette-recorders for loading programs into microcomputers. Disc drives are faster, though considerably more expensive.

The final aspect of the learner's physical environment is the terminal. The keyboard must be large enough to allow easy use (younger children require particular care here). The screen, too, must be large enough to allow comfortable reading. There must be no glare or reflection from lighting or other equipment in the room, and the screen must be at a suitable – and safe – distance from the user's eyes (a factor of special importance with colour monitors). A less obvious problem is the arrangement for text or graphics display. Basically there are two possibilities: positive or negative presentation. Black-on-white is an example of positive presentation, and green-on-black is an example of negative presentation. The green-on-black arrangement has frequently been favoured as more restful for the human eye. While this may be the case if the user is working exclusively with the computer screen, it is not the case if it is necessary to keep switching between a written paper document and the screen. The reason for this is simple. Under these circumstances, the human eye must continually refocus in order to switch from a negative (screen) to a positive (paper document) presentation. CALL packages will, of course, vary in their use of accompanying written materials. However, many packages are self-sufficient in this respect, so the problem does not arise. Working for long periods of time at a VDU can be tiring. But most teachers would in any case, on educational grounds, prefer CALL materials to be used in short sessions.

4.1.2 Using the program

The second area in CALL where ergonomics plays a role is in operating the program itself. Basic operating instructions (starting, running and leaving the program) and general keyboard procedures should be clearly documented and readily available. When the programs involve a delay – for instance, while information is being read from floppy disc or cassette – the student must be informed of the reason. Otherwise, users may switch off the equipment thinking that something has gone wrong. It is important that the learner should have no difficulty in finding the chosen package and getting it to run. For microcomputers this means making sure that the discs or cassettes are clearly labelled, and then that the instructions for inserting the disc or cassette are prominently displayed, for instance, on a noticeboard which is readily visible. Once the disc or cassette is physically in place, the instructions for loading the program into the computer must be easy to follow.

The problems on a mainframe computer are of a different nature, although the eventual aim is the same as that for microcomputers – to make it as easy as possible for the learner to gain access to a particular package. Again, instructions to the user should be explicit but not burdensome. It is preferable for instructions about getting into the system and running particular programs to be permanently displayed near the VDU, since learners may lose or forget instructions given in any other form.

Once the contents of the disc or cassette have been loaded, or the system accessed, the learner needs further guidance. In one approach, information is presented on the screen in the form of a menu from which the appropriate option is selected, as in a multiple-choice question. For example, the computer can display instructions like:

> The following programs are available:
> 1. wordorder
> 2. vocabtest
> 3. treasure
> Just type the number of the program you want

A different way of informing the user is to give the information in the form of a printed notice or a handout. The dangers are, however, fairly obvious. The noticeboard can become overcrowded and the handout may be lost.

Easy access to the program must be matched by an easy exit. Learners become frustrated if they cannot end the program when it suits them. Some programs will end the run at any time as soon as the user types 'quit'. Other programs give options at strategic points throughout the program. This may lead to complete exit from the program, or to an automatic transfer to the next section.

When designing a CALL package, one of the factors to be considered is the amount of typing required from the learner. The minimal response is a single character, usually in the context of a multiple-choice format. Some CALL programs require parts of words as answers, for example, inflectional endings. Many simply require one-word answers. Obviously, the greater the amount of typing, the more likely are keyboard errors. Computer systems all have means of correcting typing errors, whether single characters or whole lines. Instructions about the correction of errors are probably best displayed outside the program, since there is no *one* place in the program when the instructions would be relevant.

The final point here is a very important one. Many CALL users are puzzled (to say the least) when apparently correct answers are not accepted by the computer. Such occurrences are usually the result of the computer's literal-mindedness, particularly with regard to the use of the spacebar. Some examples will illustrate this point. Say the correct answer in an exercise is 'SIX PEOPLE'. The learner may answer:

> SIX   PEOPLE   [extra space between words]
> 6 PEOPLE
>   SIX PEOPLE   [initial space]
> SIX
> six people
> (etc.)

In some CALL programs, none of these answers would be accepted as correct. Such problems are discussed in sections 4.4.1 and 5.2.3. The use of upper-case versus lower-case characters, as in the last response, should be made clear for learners. Some microcomputer systems and some VDUs have only upper-case, though increasingly lower-case is available as well. This is a particular problem with mainframe computer terminals, where the same program may be used from different types of terminal. The important thing is that programs should not fail to run simply because the student uses the 'wrong form', for example, 'yes' instead of 'YES'; both should be catered for. This is really something which needs to be taken care of within the computer program. Other solutions, such as instructions to the learner on the screen, tend to be very cumbersome.

Near the beginning of this section, we said that most of the points discussed here were a matter of common sense. It is our opinion, however, that this 'common sense' often only emerges after long and sometimes bitter experience.

4.2 Natural language and the computer

The complexity of natural language is frequently underestimated, presumably because as human beings we are all more or less proficient at using one particular form of it, for example, English, Urdu, Tagalog, Swahili, as our native language. On the other hand, the complexity of machine languages is frequently overestimated, probably because of the mystique which surrounds computers. The problems of overcoming this discrepancy are most directly confronted in machine translation (section 3.4). The problem must also be faced in any CALL program, and indeed in CAL in general.

4.2.1 The complexity of natural language

Machine languages are much less complex than any natural language. A programming language for a computer is really no more than a set of unambiguous instructions for processing data (see sections 6.2 and 6.3). Where the data to be processed are in the form of natural language, certain constraints are imposed on its use, since natural language does not operate in terms of one-to-one unambiguous relationships. So in what way is natural language more complex than a machine language?

Let us look first at some of the formal properties of natural language. It is complex in the sense that it operates at a number of levels. We can illustrate this by discussing the relationship between meaning and structure. Consider the following three examples:

(1) The wolf is hard to bite.
(2) The wolf is eager to bite.
(3) The wolf is nasty to bite.
(adapted from Cromer 1970)

The structure of each example is identical:

> noun phrase + *is* + adjective + infinitive

However, although *the wolf* is the grammatical subject in all three examples, the semantic relationship between *the wolf* and the action of biting is quite different. In (1), the wolf is being bitten, in (2) it is doing the biting, whereas in (3) either interpretation is possible. Here we have an example where identical constituent structures serve for different underlying meanings. Conversely, examples (4) and (5) below exhibit different surface structures, although any native speaker of English will know that they are clearly closely related in meaning:

> (4) The dog has bitten the man.
> noun phrase + auxiliary + past participle + noun phrase
> (5) The man has been bitten.
> noun phrase + auxiliary + *been* + past participle +
> by the dog
> prepositional phrase

In other words, as human beings we perform processing operations which are far more complex than matching strings of characters, or words (which is what machines are good at). In natural language, rules do not operate on words or arbitrary strings of words, but on syntactic categories: they are structure-dependent (see Chomsky 1976:30–3 from which the following examples are taken). Consider, for example, the operation involved in converting a statement into a question, as in (6) and (7) below:

> (6) The man is tall.
> (7) Is the man tall?

This seems straightforward enough. The principle appears to be that the copula verb is moved to the beginning of the sentence. Now consider how (8) is to be made into a question:

> (8) The man who is tall is in the room.

If we move the first copula verb we come across to the beginning of the sentence, we get (9):

> (9)* is the man who tall is in the room?

Since (9) is clearly unacceptable, the rule is in obvious need of revision. We must recognize that the first *is* is part of an embedded relative clause structure *who is tall* and so is not eligible for the interrogative movement rule. In order to pick out the main rather than the first verb, we must be aware of sentence structure at some level of consciousness.

A more obvious problem than those we have already described has to do with homonymy, or roughly speaking, with cases where two words with different meanings have the same form. Examples are *bank* (financial institution) and *bank* (side of a river). Another variant of this is the homograph, for example, *lead* (for a dog) and *lead* (metal), where the words are distinguished in speech, but not in writing – a particular problem in English. Again, the lack of a one-to-one relationship between form and meaning, this time at word level, presents difficulties for a very literal-minded machine.

Another feature of natural language which is notoriously difficult for the computer to handle is anaphora. This is reflected in the relatively late acquisition by children of certain aspects of English pronominal reference (Chomsky 1969:108). Consider the following examples:

(10) John knew that he was going to win the race.
(11) He knew that John was going to win the race.

In example (10) the subject pronoun *he* can refer to *John* or to someone else. In example (11), however, the subject pronoun *he* can only refer to someone else.

Natural language is also distinguished from computer languages by its high degree of redundancy. In other words, natural language often gives us more than one indicator as to the grammatical function of a word or phrase in context. Consider the following examples:

(12) He goes to bed at six o'clock.
(13) He go to bed at six o'clock.
(14) He go bed six o'clock.

Even example (14) is still comprehensible. We regularly omit such grammatical morphemes when we write telegrams. Such omissions are also characteristic of the early stages of language development in children.

Computer languages, however, have simple and invariant rules of syntax. And they have a low degree of redundancy. For instance, if the computer received the instruction: A B, instead of: A=B, this would be a 'fatal' syntax error; the computer would not understand what was meant. However, examples (13) and (14) show that omissions, or even additions, need not be 'fatal' to the syntax of natural language.

4.2.2 Implementing dialogue

So far we have talked about meaning in natural language in isolated sentences. When we look at natural language in the form of a continuous written text or as a tool of human interaction, the picture becomes even more complex. For instance, inference plays an important part in our understanding of language and enables us to connect facts which have no linguistic link. In the following example, there is no structural or semantic link between Mary being away from school and the fact that her mother was ill:

(15) Mary wasn't at school today. Her mother was ill.

However, any speaker of English will be able to draw the inference that Mary's mother's illness was the reason for her absence (cf. Lehnert & Ringle 1982).

No dialogue, beyond very ritualized exchanges, is predictable in a narrow sense, since we have a potentially infinite number of permutations at our disposal in terms of intended meaning, structure and vocabulary. In a wider sense, discourse can of course be described in the way it is structured (Sinclair & Coulthard 1975), but the exact words the next speaker is going to use cannot be predicted. Nevertheless, some work is going on in this area. For instance, GUIDON, a program being developed at Stanford for teaching diagnostic problem-solving to medical students, aims to use 'prolonged, structured teaching interactions that go beyond responding to the student's last move' (Barr & Feigenbaum 1982:267). Another program which gives some indication of the potential for text-understanding by computers is POLITICS. This uses inference to reply to questions input by the user (Schank 1979:216–17). However, the range of knowledge on which this inference is based is extremely limited in comparison to that of human beings. A 'language understanding program' has also been written by Winograd (1972), using the computer programming languages LISP and PLANNER. His program attempts to deal with the different aspects of normal language usage (syntax, semantics and inference) in an integrated way. For instance, the left-to-right operation of the parsing system, whose job it is to identify structural patterns and recognize their relevant features, can be interrupted so that other semantic or syntactic computations can be performed. Winograd gives the example of the 'semantic analyzer' establishing that the string of words *the street in a car* is not a possible constituent in the sentence: *I rode down the street in a car* (Winograd 1972:21–3). Another important point about Winograd's approach is the emphasis he places on the importance of knowledge about the world in understanding language. This has been built into his program, but of necessity, the world the computer is programmed to 'know' is limited to 'a simple scene containing a table, hand, and box, and several blocks and pyramids' (Winograd 1972:8). It will obviously be a huge jump to extend such a program, already highly complex, to a more interesting 'world'. Another example of the computer's ability to carry on a dialogue about a highly restricted environment is

SOPHIE, a 'computer tutor' which teaches trainees to detect faults in electronic circuits (O'Shea & Self 1983:162–9). The grammar operates in semantic categories which are specifically related to the subject area. It is also capable of dealing with some examples of ellipsis and pronominal reference.

While it is not possible for the computer to cope with open-ended dialogue, there are nevertheless ways in which a dialogue can be simulated (see for instance Weizenbaum's well-known ELIZA program, Weizenbaum 1976:1–17). This can be further developed by the inclusion of various human characteristics such as friendliness and informality (see Johns's 'snuggle-up routine', 1981:99–100), politeness or irritation. For instance, where the user types in an answer which the computer program cannot deal with, a standard response can be used. Instead of the VDU showing a bald response such as 'ER!' or '?', one of the following could appear:

SORRY. DIDN'T UNDERSTAND. HAVE ANOTHER GO.   (informal)
YOU MUST HAVE MADE A MISTAKE. I DIDN'T UNDERSTAND.
PLEASE TRY AGAIN.   (polite)
IDIOT. YOU'VE MADE A MISTAKE. TRY AGAIN.   (irritation)

In these examples all that is necessary is a different line of text in the program.

However, making a computer appear to behave like a human being may have certain disadvantages. For one thing, anthropomorphic fantasies about the computer are not universal (Farrington 1981). Furthermore, such an approach may exaggerate the user's belief in the computer's ability to carry on a real dialogue. Finally, for some more complex routines, the program author may expend a considerable amount of energy for uncertain returns.

4.3   Natural language and the learner

Some advances could be made in the production of successful language-teaching materials if these were based on an understanding of how human beings learn language. While such a condition may seem self-evident, the practice of language teaching in its various guises has historically paid scant attention to this fundamental question. Indeed, research in this area has only just begun to make progress.

4.3.1   Recent developments

In the last two decades our view of language learning has changed considerably. The audio-lingual teaching methods of the 1960s rested on the assumption that foreign-language learning was psychologically a question of learning new habits, and that linguistically this amounted to learning new structures. Even transformational-generative grammar had little effect on the nature of language-teaching courses, despite its massive impact on theoretical linguistics and on research into child language acquisition. Bell (1981:76) suggests that the reason for its lack of impact on second-language teaching was a continued preoccupation with form, or 'the mastery of a decontextualized code'. He goes on to claim that since the early 1970s a new approach has emerged which focuses on language as 'social behaviour'. This refers of course to the notional/functional syllabuses which have been emerging since the mid 1970s and which focus on 'communicative competence'. Speech Act Theory (Austin 1962; Searle 1969) has had an important influence on this development. It is argued that language which concentrates on form ignores the function to which particular utterances are put. For example, while the meaning of a sentence may be clear, the use to which it is put is only evident in a specified context: so, is the sentence *He'll see you later* a warning (*to tell you off*) or a promise (*to buy you lunch*)? In Searle's terms, language which concentrates purely on form is not 'serious language'.

This presents some difficulties for CALL: we have already indicated in section 4.2 that the outlook for using computers in meaningful or 'serious' dialogue is limited. CALL's place in the language classroom is not that of a spontaneous dialogue partner in either the written or the spoken medium.

4.3.2 A model of language learning

While certain ideas have filtered through to the language-teaching classroom from the philosophy of language (speech acts) and sociolinguistics (communicative competence), psycholinguistic research appears to have had little impact to date. 'Theories of language learning' have in the past been little more than – theoretically or empirically – unsubstantiated suggestions for language-teaching methodology. The early 1970s saw a surge of empirical research in naturalistic second-language acquisition, although little empirical work has been carried out until recently on language learning in a formal situation like the classroom.

What are the main findings of this psycholinguistic research? It seems that first-language background has much less to do with the linguistic development of second-language learners than was originally thought – at least in syntax and morphology. The influence of the first language appears to be strongest in phonology. Other findings relate to the role of motivation and personality factors in the eventual success or failure to learn, and to the ability of learners to self-edit their language output; these last two factors have been referred to as the 'Affective Filter' and the 'Monitor' respectively (Dulay, Burt & Krashen 1982:4).

Krashen's Monitor Model is well known (Krashen 1977; 1978). He makes a case for a distinction between a conscious process of language learning and a subconscious process of language acquisition. The latter, he claims, is typical of children acquiring first and second languages, whereas the process of learning is only available after the onset of Piaget's formal operational period at about twelve years (Krashen 1981:34–5). When the emphasis is on the message, the learner is 'acquiring'; when the emphasis is on form, then 'learning' is going on. So the 'acquisition' process, in Krashen's usage, does not demonstrably benefit from overt correction or presentation of explicit rules, whereas the 'learning' process does. Krashen's model claims that language production is initiated by the learner's 'acquired' system. The output of this system is then 'monitored' by the 'learned' system, given certain conditions such as time for reflection, focus on form, and knowledge of the rules. The 'optimal Monitor user' appears to be the learner who manages to balance the demands of message and form. This is the student who does not fail to produce language for fear of making errors (the 'overuser') and who does not produce totally unedited strings of language without regard to errors (the 'underuser').

4.3.3 Medium versus message

While the study of grammar alone has been shown to be insufficient as a preparation for communicating, this does not mean that explicit knowledge of grammar is unnecessary if the student wishes to be a 'good language learner'. Nor does a mentalist (rule-based) framework for language acquisition, as opposed to a behaviourist (habit formation) approach, exclude the obvious benefits of practice and repetition. The emphasis has simply shifted. Many teachers now prefer to give more weight to the 'message' or 'comprehensible input'. However, that is not to say that we should not also provide students with opportunities for 'learning' in Krashen's sense. CALL is one of the resources which can fulfil this requirement.

Furthermore, learning (explicit attention to rules) as opposed to acquisition does not have to be associated exclusively with the behaviouristic model of language acquisition, the drilling of habits based on a contrastive analysis of the learner's L1 and L2, which was so strongly favoured through the 1960s and early 1970s. Johns (1983:93), for instance, has investigated ways of using CALL to give students the opportunity 'to form appropriate hypotheses and guess intelligently'. He emphasizes the importance of cognitive skills in the development of strategies for language learning. Another feature of his programs is that they are largely text-based; this means that they put greater emphasis on meaning.

The distinction between message and form in second-language acquisition has also been made by Dodson on the basis of the Schools Council bilingual teaching programmes he studied in Wales (1978). Dodson formulates this distinction in terms of 'message-orientated' versus 'medium-orientated' language. His observations refer to children beginning Welsh as a second language from the age of five years. He notes that 'many teachers initially made the error of expecting message-orientated communication without the initial first-level medium-orientated work for any given play activity' (1978:48). He concludes that: 'There was thus a direct connection between the pupils' ability to make use of language in true communicative situations and the teacher's methodological sequencing' (1978:49). Hawkins describes this as 're-hearsal' (medium) for 'performance' (message). He distinguishes a range of language-learning exercises which cover both 'rehearsal' and 'performance' (1981:213–14, 246–7, 252–72). Littlewood also distinguishes between 'pre-communicative' and communicative activities, where pre-communicative refers to the production of language forms (1981:16). So although the relationship between form and communication suggested here is different from that suggested by Krashen, the need for a range of learning activities and environments is again acknowledged.

An interesting feature of Hawkins's suggested design for the modern-language curriculum in secondary schools is the importance he attaches to 'language awareness' training. This is a broad programme which draws on many aspects of linguistics. He sees this as a joint enterprise to be undertaken by mother-tongue and foreign-language teachers (1981:292–306). Such projects are already under way (Jenkins 1980; Aplin, Crawshaw, Roselman & Williams 1981). It seems to us that an imaginative use can be made of CAL in this field, although little work has yet been carried out. Such programs might be factually orientated (language families) or discovery orientated (importance of word order, relationships between words, importance of word endings). Various approaches can be adopted: the computer as a source of information; the computer as a tester of the student; the computer as a tool to manipulate examples ('try-it-and-see' approach). Some interesting work in this field has already been started with primary school children in Edinburgh (Sharples 1981a; 1981b) where the aim of the project is to help the children 'understand language and develop their writing style' through manipulation of grammar and vocabulary using the computer.

4.3.4 Styles of learning

So far we have talked about the learner as a psychologically uniform being. 'The learner' is obviously more complex than that. While broad patterns of development are shared by all learners, there is evidence that learners do have different 'styles' of learning. Bruner (1966) points out that particular domains of knowledge may be represented to the learner in different ways in order to facilitate learning. This may vary not only with the subject matter, but also with the style of the learner. In first-language acquisition variations in learning style have also been acknowledged. Ramer (1976) has suggested that girls and boys learning English as a first language employ different learning strategies in some areas. In second-language acquisition reference is often made to different 'types' of learner, although unfortunately the point is rarely amplified. For instance, Clahsen (1980) refers to 'rhetorically expressive learners' versus 'error preventers'; elsewhere, Hatch (1974) talks of 'data-gatherers' versus 'rule-formers', and Taylor (1975) reports Brown's (1973) distinction between 'reflective' and 'impulsive' learners. Given that there are different styles of learning, a variety of approaches is required. Working with a computer appeals more to some learners than to others, and particular program types have different degrees of success with various students.

4.3.5 Summary

We have seen how the trend in language teaching has been away from form towards function and communicative skills. Nonetheless, there is a strong body of opinion which still emphasizes the need for teaching of language form. This is something which CALL can do well, either as directed practice for the learner, or as an exploratory exercise in language manipulation. Since psycholinguistic evidence about the way or ways in which human beings learn language is not yet far advanced, we can probably do no better at this stage than to offer learners a range of activities suited to different cognitive styles. CALL is capable of covering the whole range from expository teaching to discovery learning. Finally, it may be that particular learners enjoy working with a machine – others may not. This is a personality factor which needs to be borne in mind.

4.4 Review of the triangle

Our analysis of the relationship of learner, language and computer, on which CALL is based, has served to highlight the problems as well as the possibilities for CALL. We have already considered approaches to some of the problems. In this section we draw together the threads of our discussion and carry it a little further forward. The three factors – learner, language and computer – will continue to be central to the argument throughout the rest of the book.

4.4.1 Ergonomic considerations

The important points which the teacher should consider about the physical environment of the learner are:

(a) location of computer or terminal
(b) student access (booking system)
(c) comfort for working (chair; table etc.)
(d) time taken to start program (cassette versus disc)
(e) ease of reading (screen size and presentation)

Point (a) may be a decision already made for the teacher in his or her institution. Nevertheless, some of the pedagogical implications of locating the computer or terminal in the classroom or in a laboratory are worth consideration (see section 7.4). The implementation of a booking system (point b) is, however, clearly within the teacher's control. The student's comfort (point c) may be within the teacher's sphere of influence, if not within direct control. Points (d) and (e) are subject to financial constraints, but when asked for an opinion about which equipment to buy, teachers should bear these questions in mind.

The ergonomic problems associated with operating the actual package are probably most acute with inexperienced computer users. Nonetheless, it is wise to cater primarily for this group, since they will never gain experience if their initial attempts at running programs are disastrous. Some ground rules are offered here for designing or evaluating CALL materials:

(f) make the conventions for formulating answers to the computer as clear as possible
(g) take advantage of flexible matching procedures for checking answers where appropriate
(h) avoid lengthy typing within student answers
(i) make it easy to start the CALL program
(j) allow student choice about when to exit from the CALL program

In making input conventions clear to the user, the program author should try not to let such considerations interfere with the main purpose of the package. Long explanations in the text about the dangers of overusing the spacebar, or when to use upper-case characters only, and so on, are to be avoided. Such instructions simply clutter up a package. Prophylactic action is preferred and can be taken by providing clear examples of the format which is expected of the student in the answer or enquiry, preliminary practice, or by providing a repeated instruction immediately before the student responds (point f). The latter may, however, become rather tedious for the student. If prophylaxis fails, then flexible matching routines (for instance, fuzzy matching, pattern markup, instring search, see section 5.2.3) are a good back-up. These must of course be selectively used according to the type of exercise in question, for instance, spelling or comprehension (point g).

Requiring the student to type in long answers should be avoided simply for the reason that it increases the likelihood of error. Concentrating on manual skills may seriously detract from the purpose of the package and may also lead to a high degree of frustration (point h). There are, however, ways of dealing with longer answers or enquiries. Students may be asked to choose between two or more alternative responses, to reply 'yes' or 'no', 'more' or 'less', 'bigger' or 'smaller' and so on, to a series of questions. In an even simpler way, students can be instructed to type in only the initial letter of their answer or enquiry. For instance, if the package is designed to give information about the rules for gender assignment in French, the student can be told to type in 'm' or 'f' if information is required about masculine or feminine nouns. A further alternative is provided by the touch-sensitive screen (see section 3.1.2) or the 'mouse' (see section 1.3).

While point (i) about making the program easy to start is obvious, point (j) may seem less so. Why bother about helping a captive audience to leave your magnificent program? The answer is simply that students get very frustrated if they cannot leave a program. There is a certain degree of resentment involved in being held captive by a machine. Program authors must therefore build in options to exit at appropriate points. It is also possible to let the student have a single command which will enable him or her to escape at any time (see section 5.2.6).

4.4.2 *Linguistic considerations*

In section 4.2 we pointed out the difficulties which natural-language input poses for computers: the lack of isomorphism between meaning and form, ellipsis, the range of structural choice, the role of prior knowledge about the world, the expression of irony, humour, lies, inference, and so on. These are all features of natural language which human beings deal with in a fairly efficient way, but which pose enormous problems for a machine. If we wish to use CALL for practising or evaluating productive use of language, then the following point must apply:

(k) avoid exercises where open-ended production of language by the learner is required as input to the computer

Some teachers may now want to stop reading; this would be a mistake. Point (k) does not mean that all types of exercise except those which require grammatically clear-cut and brief answers are ruled out. We simply have to use the computer in a different way (for instance, to stimulate discussion, see section 7.2.4) or to rely on other techniques for processing input from the learner, more suited to the computer's literal-mindedness (for instance, multiple-choice, see section 7.2.3).

CALL programs still have to be so literal because there is to date no CALL system which can fully process semantically the learner's unrestricted written input. The problem lies in the software. CALL programs as they exist currently are linguistically primitive in the sense that they enable the computer to respond only to pre-programmed learner input which is anticipated and expected by the program author. CALL programs are not yet intelligent enough to cope adequately with the complexities of natural-language processing (see section 3.3).

So far we have concentrated on the processing of written language. The computer can accept and respond to (restricted) written input from the user, and it can also output written language on the VDU or in hard copy through a printer (see section 6.4.1). However, the spoken medium is much more limited. Speech output is available on some systems using a variety of techniques (see section 8.4). This usually involves the reproduction of recorded material (digitized or on conventional tape) while a few advanced systems offer speech synthesis. The point to stress, however, is that the computer's speech output comes as a response to the learner's written input. When we consider the question of spoken input to the computer, our options become even fewer. There is at present no low-cost system which can accept normal speech input, although some speech-recognition systems in highly specified contexts are under development, and are already functioning in some commercial applications. To date, however, there is no commercially available CALL system where speech recognition is used to check the learner's answer (some of the pedagogical implications are discussed in section 7.2.1). So the next point to remember is:

(l) do not expect the computer to process speech input

Generally speaking, then, CALL is still forced to concentrate on the written medium, although speech output is available to a limited extent. And spontaneous interaction with the computer is ruled out. However, both of these points, while restrictive in one sense, will force us to explore ways of expanding our language-teaching activities using the computer's special capabilities (see section 7.2.4). This is surely preferable to lamenting the fact that the computer cannot match the teacher at interactive dialogue. Indeed, such an objective seems in many ways misplaced, although written dialogue is an essential feature of program operation, not only in CALL, but in CAL in general.

4.4.3 Pedagogic considerations

It is not clear how human beings learn language. However, current thinking emphasizes the following three points (Dulay, Burt & Krashen 1982):

(m) provide the learner with an opportunity to use language 'to mean'
(n) encourage a positive attitude on the part of the learner
(o) provide opportunities for learning without anxiety

Let us deal briefly with points (n) and (o) first. It is difficult to associate either point with a specific feature of CALL. We shall simply refer to the apparent enjoyment of learners using CALL (often regardless of the type of exercise presented – at least initially). Such enjoyment must contribute to a positive attitude to the activity of learning and to the subject matter (see section 7.5). The privacy which CALL can provide must also be a factor in lowering anxiety levels (see section 7.3). Learning may therefore be encouraged through increased motivation and self-confidence. However, it is important to remember that monitoring may be counter-productive in this respect.

We saw in the previous chapter that one of CALL's historical predecessors, programmed instruction, was closely associated with behaviourist theories of learning. Point (m) is clearly based in quite a different framework. In many respects, CALL is still the pedagogical descendant of programmed instruction. This is reinforced by some of the technological and linguistic limitations indicated earlier in this chapter. However, it must be stressed that CALL is not inherently associated with any specific methodology. So what should we do in the meantime while those working in artificial intelligence try to narrow the gap between machine and language? We can do two things:

(p) improve conventional exercises
(q) explore ways of harnessing the computer's special capabilities

Point (p) requires intelligent use of features already available on the computer: scoring, error correction, feedback on errors, contextualization of answers, options for help, step-by-step answers, flexible matching routines, and so on (as will be discussed in chapter 5). One of the best ways of improving conventional exercises is to build in **branching structures**, where the learner does not follow a single straight path through the material (a **linear program structure**), but pursues different paths according to choices and responses made in the course of the session. A further alternative, which can be either integrated into a practice program (as a help facility), or used as a separate program, is the computer as **oracle**. In this mode, the student interrogates the computer, not vice versa. A simple example of this technique is to be found in RUNEX (Ahmad, Colenso & Corbett 1978).

This leads to consideration of ways of expanding CALL activities beyond sophisticated versions of conventional exercises (point q), characteristic of a tutorial mode. The computer need not always play the role of censorious, or even helpful teacher. It may also act as a source of various types of information to the student. The conventional way of using the computer as oracle is as a source of factual information, as described above. However, there are possibilities for extending this mode. **Simulation** programs, for example, enable the user to manipulate a given situation or set of data in order to test the outcome of a decision; this can encompass changing the variables in a real-life or imaginary situation, or performing manipulations on words or text to test the outcome. **Generative** programs take advantage of the computer's ability to produce phrases or sentences on the basis of a limited corpus and a set of rules; **heuristic** programs enable the learner to expand the computer's stock of 'knowledge'. These possibilities, and others, are explored in more detail in section 7.2.4. Any of these more innovative program types, and indeed more traditional types of language exercise, can also be presented in the form of a game. It is worth noting that a game format is simply a method of presenting the CALL package and is not a particular type of program in itself.

In simulation, manipulation and generative-type programs, there really are no right or wrong answers; the computer is simply providing information for the learner to evaluate. Such programs are obviously not suitable for scoring or monitoring (see section 7.3). It is also difficult to quantify their value. This type of exercise allows the learner freedom to explore. It also takes advantage of the very feature which was a constraining factor in the type of exercise indicated in point (p) – the computer's literal-mindedness and its need for structural precision. Manipulating or generating language in a mechanical way is something which human beings find rather hard. They find it particularly difficult to be thorough and exhaustive in considering all possible permutations. This is precisely what the computer is good at.

4.5   Conclusion

We began by exploring some ways in which learners can be encouraged in their use of CALL by taking into account various factors in the physical environment and in actually running the programs. Of a more theoretical nature are the problems posed for the computer by natural language. What is needed is software which is capable of semantic analysis of natural language. Such work is still in its early stages. Finally, we turned to some of the fundamental issues in language learning and teaching, with particular reference to CALL. Many of the points which relate to learning and teaching are still the subject of fierce dispute among classroom practitioners generally, so it is not surprising that CALL is caught in the same crossfire. Some of the factors discussed here present serious challenges for CALL, particularly at its present stage of development. We have attempted to indicate reasonable answers to the challenges, as well as showing the way ahead. Several of the questions considered here in theoretical terms are tackled on the basis of a practical example in the next chapter.

5 An example: GERAD

In this chapter we take a close look at a particular CALL package called GERAD, an example of CALL used in tutorial mode. We examine what it does and consider different approaches to a well-defined problem of language teaching. The package was produced by two of the authors in 1978. It is not presented as a model CALL package, but rather as a package with some interesting features and reasonable for its time. It lacks some of the refinements of more recent packages, but its clear structure will serve well as the basis for a discussion of essential techniques. We will consider the purpose for which GERAD was designed (section 5.1), then go through a run of the package step by step, as it appears to the learner (section 5.2). There follows a brief account of the technical details of the program (section 5.3) and then a review of its main features (section 5.4). As we go through, there are two questions worth bearing in mind: first, would you tackle this problem in this way? and second (though the package is not actually available commercially) would you buy it?

5.1 The purpose of the package

The package was designed to tackle a problem posed by the GERman ADjective (hence GERAD), namely the ending required when it stands in attributive position. The adjective agrees in gender, number and case with the noun. There is a further complication, in that the form to be used depends also on whether the noun phrase contains a determiner and furthermore, on the type of determiner involved. We find examples like:

> (1) ein guter Mann
>   a   good   man

Mann is masculine singular, and here stands in the nominative case; this combination of features requires the ending *-er* on *guter*. Compare this with a similar phrase where the definite article is present:

> (2) der gute Mann
>   the good man

In (2) the *-er* ending on the determiner results from the features masculine, singular and nominative, and this information is not repeated on the adjective. The adjective has two sets of endings, the 'strong' endings (as in (1)), and the 'weak' endings (as in (2)), though these overlap to a considerable extent. The correct choice of ending is a real problem for students of German. This was demonstrated by an error analysis of examination essays written by first-year undergraduate students, who had had at least four years' formal tuition in German. Of a total of 698 errors found, nearly 5 per cent (33 in fact) involved incorrect adjectival endings; this was the seventh largest single source of error (Rogers 1984). The GERAD package had been originally intended for near beginners in the language; it was subsequently found to be of value for remedial work for more advanced learners, whose need for such additional material is clearly shown by these figures.

5.2 The package in use

Let us assume that a student (or pair of students, since many CALL packages are particularly effective when tackled co-operatively) is sitting at a VDU ready to use the package. This may be in the context of a regular class, or as private practice. We will follow the student's progress through the package.

5.2.1 Initial presentation

In order to start, the student types: RUN GERAD. The command RUN is used to start all the CALL programs at Surrey, and so the student is likely to be familiar with it. The name of the program GERAD would be obtained either from a list of programs available, or the student may be specifically directed to this program by the teacher. The computer responds by offering an explanation of the problem if required. Thus, the first exchange looks like this:

> RUN GERAD [typed by the student]
>> Do you want an introduction to this program?
>> Please type YES or NO.

(What the student types is printed here two spaces to the left of the computer's contribution, to make it easier to follow the exchange.) Many packages begin with a brief account of what the package is intended to do. In the case of GERAD, the student is given the option of having a very detailed account of German adjectival endings, or of going straight to the exercise section of the package. A student using the package for the second or subsequent time would probably take the latter course. We will assume that the student types YES, opting for the explanation. In this case, the explanation is displayed on the screen, a section at a time, in blocks of about paragraph length. For example:

RUN GERAD
Do you want an introduction to this program?
Please type YES or NO.
YES
Only adjectives which precede the noun require a change in ending, e.g. DAS BUCH IST <u>ROT</u>
DAS <u>ROTE</u> BUCH
AUF DEM TISCH LIEGT EIN BUCH. ES IST <u>ROT</u>
AUF DEM TISCH LIEGT EIN <u>ROTES</u> BUCH
>>>>>> Press RETURN to continue

[student presses RETURN]
The function of the adjective endings is to give as much information as is necessary to indicate the case, gender and number (singular or plural) of the noun to which the adjective refers. For instance, in the following examples we can see from the definite article (DER) that the noun phrase (article + adjective + noun) is nominative, masculine singular:
DER NEUE PULLOVER
>>>>>>> Press RETURN to continue

The part of the explanation which the student is reading remains on the screen until the RETURN key is pressed. This has two advantages: it allows the student to go through the explanation at his or her own speed, re-reading or skimming sections where necessary; it also draws attention to the RETURN key, which must be pressed before the computer responds to any of the student's input. The explanation is couched in functional terms, and therefore gives students a different perspective from that provided by the majority of textbooks. Nevertheless it was not intended that this should be the student's introduction to the problem; rather, it would be a revision of something the student had already met in the classroom – recently in the case of beginners, further in the past for the more advanced students. It is worth pointing out that text of this type can be modified easily, without affecting the main part of the program. If experience shows that a particular part of the explanation is confusing, too advanced or too trivial for a given set of users, then it can readily be revised. This process of gradual improvement is one of the important features of work in CALL. The explanation at the beginning of GERAD is rather long, comprising discussion of the principles involved in the choice of adjectival ending, full paradigms using different lexical items to show the various combinations of endings, reduced paradigms with just the two sets of endings (weak and strong) and, of course, numerous examples throughout. It takes several minutes to work through the explanation.

5.2.2 Asking a question

Once the student reaches the end of the explanation (or right at the beginning of the session if the explanation is omitted), the computer puts the first question, in the following format (the English gloss provided below does not appear on the screen):

Fill in the blank:
ICH SUCHE EIN ZIMMER MIT _____ WASSER.   <FLIESSEND>
[I look for a room with   water   running]
If help required type HILFE, otherwise give your answer.

This sentence means 'I am looking for a room with _____ water'. The adjective *fliessend*, which the student is to insert in the gap, means 'running'; *Hilfe* is the German for 'help'. The student has to work out which set of endings is required (strong or weak), the gender, number and case of the noun, and from these, the actual ending. The exercise need not be presented in this way. The different operations could be practised separately: the student could be told the gender, number and so on, without a contextualized example, and merely asked to give the correct ending – in other words, the question would be asked in straight grammatical terms. Alternatively, the task could be made more difficult by setting questions in German, the answers to which involved a phrase of the type required. Exercises of the latter type are notoriously difficult to devise. GERAD stands between these two possibilities: the student has to work out the grammatical information from the linguistic context, yet the required words are specified, so that there can be only one possible answer to the question.

An interesting feature of GERAD, shown in the extract above, is the help facility, which can be called on if the student does not wish to or cannot answer the question immediately. The student is asked to choose between two help messages, one for each set of adjective endings. Then the required set is displayed on the screen, together with a few words of explanation – a summary version of part of the optional introduction. This helpful material remains on the screen while the original question is repeated. The student can then use the table to help find the answer (it is still necessary to establish the gender, number and case required, but once this is done, the appropriate form can be obtained from the table). The exchange might take the following form:

Fill in the blank:
ICH SUCHE EIN ZIMMER MIT_____ WASSER. <FLIESSEND>
If help is required type HILFE, otherwise give your answer.
HILFE [student response]

Do you want help with strong or weak endings?
Type 1 for Strong, 2 for Weak.

1 [student response]
SUMMARY
Typical endings ('PRIMARY') are as follows (e.g. the typical ending for masculine dative is '-em', for neuter nominative '-es'):

★★
     MASC   FEM   NEUT   PLURAL
★★

	MASC	FEM	NEUT	PLURAL
NOM	-ER	-E	-ES(-S)	-E
ACC	-EN	-E	-ES	-E
DAT	-EM	-ER	-EM	-EN
GEN	-ES	-ER	-ES	-ER

★★
>>>>>>>>>>Press RETURN to continue

[student presses RETURN]
Fill in the blank:
ICH SUCHE EIN ZIMMER MIT _____ WASSER. <FLIESSEND>

Each fresh line of text, whether input by the student or provided by the computer, appears at the bottom of the VDU screen: all that was visible previously moves upwards and, if the screen was full, the top line disappears. The screen of a VDU can usually accommodate around twenty lines of text: there is therefore no difficulty in displaying the table and the questions together. Independently, or with some help, the student gives an answer. The computer does not respond until the RETURN key is pressed; the student can correct errors, grammatical mistakes or spelling slips, by backspacing and typing the desired version in place of the original attempt. When satisfied, he or she presses RETURN, and the computer responds.

It is possible to set a timer to limit the length of time spent on any question. The timer can be set for, say, ten seconds, after which the student has no further chance to answer the question, or it can first give a warning followed by a second short answer period. The timer is particularly useful when CALL packages are used for testing purposes. GERAD is clearly designed for learning: the student should work out the factors involved in the choice of adjectival endings, using the help facility when necessary; if, therefore, a student were to spend several minutes considering the answer to a single question, this would not worry the authors of the package at all; they had no desire to determine how long a student could spend on particular questions, and so did not use a timer. Of course, CALL packages should be judged by the time the learner spends in useful learning, and certainly not by the amount of computer processing time used.

5.2.3 Assessing the answer

Once the student has responded, the computer checks the answer. If it is correct, this is confirmed and the full sentence is repeated, including the adjective in the form given by the student. Then the exercise continues. But if the answer is incorrect, this is pointed out, and the correct form is given, as follows:

> Fill in the blank:
> ICH SUCHE EIN ZIMMER MIT _____ WASSER. <FLIESSEND>
> FLIESSENDEN [student response]
> Your answer is incorrect.
> The correct answer is ::::::
> FLIESSENDEM
> The correct sentence is:
> ICH SUCHE EIN ZIMMER MIT FLIESSENDEM WASSER.

Thus, in either case, the last form displayed on the screen is the correct one. While the response to correct answers requires little comment, the handling of errors is worth considering further. GERAD checks only for an exact match. Thus the correct form in the sentence given is *FLIESSEN-DEM*. Any other form will simply be deemed incorrect, whether it is a 'near miss', a form wide of the mark, or a completely improbable answer.

An alternative is to check for particular incorrect answers, anticipating errors that the student may make. For example, we could check for the strong ending when the weak ending is required and vice versa. Thus in the sentence above, we could check not only for *FLIESSENDEM* (strong: correct) but also for *FLIESSENDEN* (weak: incorrect). If the student gave the answer *FLIESSENDEN* a message would be printed, for example: 'No, that is the weak form. When there is no determiner the strong form is required. Try again.' Thus we are checking first for the right answer, then for a specific (predictable) wrong answer, sometimes called a **trapped error**: anything else is simply treated as incorrect. This method has distinct advantages, provided the source of the error is clear. However, this is frequently not the case. In the example above, for example, the incorrect answer *FLIESSENDEN* could convincingly result from a student incorrectly using the commonest ending. Of course it is possible to investigate the reason for the error step by step: 'What is the gender of the noun?', 'What case does the preposition *mit* take?' and so on. And one can check for various incorrect answers rather than just one (the place of anticipating errors in monitoring is taken up in section 7.3).

Instead of checking only for certain exactly specified answers, a technique known as **fuzzy matching** can be used. When the student's answer is checked against the expected answer, it is deemed to match if it corresponds to a specified degree. It is possible to control the closeness of match required, and in a number of different ways. This technique would not be appropriate for GERAD, since GERAD is concerned with exact understanding of a small number of inflections; by the very nature of the learning task, fuzzy matching would be self-defeating. But suppose we have a comprehension exercise – say a set of questions on a French passage. The answer to one of our questions is 'Jacques'. If a student makes a spelling error 'Jaques' or 'Jacque' we do not wish the computer to respond blandly 'Incorrect', as it would to the student answer 'Anne-Marie'. It should acknowledge the fact that he or she has successfully understood the point required. Fuzzy matching would allow a response from the computer such as 'Yes, it was him. But your answer contains a spelling error. Try again'; or 'Yes, it was Jacques – note the spelling.' Teachers have varying attitudes to spelling but few would be concerned about extra spaces; many programs have useful routines to disregard spaces at the beginning of answers and additional spaces between words (Kenning & Kenning 1983:120-2).

Comprehension exercises may also take advantage of a facility called **instring search**, in which the computer searches for keywords in the student's answer. This is useful in more open-ended exercises where the teacher does not wish to use a multiple-choice format or restrict the learner's input in an unrealistic way. However, program authors should be aware of certain pitfalls in this technique, such as the occurrence of negatives, so that the computer looking for the answer '... lazy ...' does not accept the answer '... not lazy ...' or '... no-one ... lazy ...'. Another technique which is particularly valuable when longer answers are required is **pattern markup**. This is better suited to exercises which are defined in a less open-ended way. The student answer is compared with the right answer and discrepancies are indicated. PLATO has an elaborate system (Hart 1981b:7–9). Suppose that the expected answer is:

This emergency exit must be left unlocked.

The student response is:

this emergincy exit must be always left undid.
↑ = = = = =   xxxxxx xxxxx

The ↑ indicates a capitalization error, = = = = a spelling mistake and xxxx a badly misspelt word or one which should not appear in the answer. There are further symbols for words appearing in the wrong position. Similar systems are becoming available on microcomputers. An important difference between pattern markup and the attempt to predict incorrect answers is that in pattern markup the same procedure is used to check every response – a single answer is stored for each question, which is more economical in preparation time. The two approaches could be combined in an attempt to secure the advantages of each. While pattern markup has advantages, it can be inaccurate and misleading if there are several similar words in the response. (For a useful review of error correction see Pusack 1983; future prospects are mentioned in section 8.3.)

To return to GERAD, we may say that the authors adopted the strictest position – only 'perfect' answers are accepted. And given that the adjective root is provided and the endings can be called for by the student, this position seems sensible. In GERAD, the student has only one attempt at each question – the correct answer is given after the first unsuccessful response. Of course, it is possible to allow two, three or four attempts, or to allow the student to keep trying as long as he or she wishes and to provide the answer only when it is asked for. Some programs give clues for multiple attempts at a question. GERAD uses the simplest option. Note too the messages: 'Your answer is correct/incorrect.' More effusive replies such as 'Well done, that is correct' soon become tedious when repeated. Some teachers prefer CALL programs not to be censorious, and indicate responses such as: 'That's not the answer I'm looking for.' Changing the text of such responses is a simple matter.

5.2.4 *Scoring*

Once the student has responded and the answer has been confirmed as correct, or the correct form displayed if the answer was wrong, the computer gives a score. It gives the student points for correct answers and awards itself points for errors, for example:

```
Your answer is correct.
**************************************************************
*         MY  POINTS        -        YOUR  POINTS           *
**************************************************************
*              0            -             1                 *
**************************************************************
```

Several aspects of scoring deserve comment. In GERAD a score is given automatically. In some CALL programs the student has a choice whether the exercise is to be scored or not. Students almost always opt to have a score, so the lack of a chance to suppress it in GERAD is no great loss. In GERAD the scoring is simple: each question is worth one point. However, if help is requested the machine gives itself a point – so the student, by getting the right answer, can only stay level when help is given. Of course, scoring systems can be made more subtle; if tasks are of unequal difficulty, this can be reflected in the number of points awarded.

GERAD does not record the scores; they are for entertainment, encouragement and guidance. As we have already mentioned, students generally like to have a score and to compete against the computer. It is

71

certainly difficult to persuade a student to leave while the machine is 'winning'. The fact that the scores are lost once the session finishes is fully consistent with the intention of GERAD as a teaching package in which the student can learn by experience. However, it is possible for CALL packages to record scores, including such details as the questions which were answered incorrectly, the time spent and so on, if required. The general question of monitoring is considered in section 7.3.

Finally, the presentation of the score on the screen is a point sometimes overlooked. It should be given an attractive layout, as it can occur many times during the run of a package. Given that the format stays the same and that the function of this part of the package is clear, it is an obvious area to transfer to the target language. Thus a second package, similar to GERAD in basic design, could score using the German *meine Punkte – deine Punkte* (one could even make the switch part-way through a run of GERAD). Similarly, phrases such as 'Your answer is correct' could be in German. In a set of Russian packages produced by two of the authors at the University of Surrey, this is done gradually so that in the most advanced package all the questions, answers and comments are in Russian. At the beginning, of course, the emphasis must be on ensuring that the student knows what is going on. Once the student is familiar with working on the computer, then the progressive introduction of the target language is a sensible step.

5.2.5   The next question

After the first question has been answered, checked and scored, the computer asks a second question. In GERAD, this is not simply the next question on a set list. GERAD has a stock of sixty sentences which are selected at random. This means that two students sitting side by side at two different terminals would encounter different sets of questions. More importantly, someone who used GERAD on one occasion and then returned at a later date, whether to try to do better or to revise the area practised, would receive a new set of questions, though some might coincide with those of the first session. The randomness of the questions is modified in two ways. First, the sixty sentences include an increased proportion of examples in which the adjective occurs in the nominative or accusative plural, because in the error-analysis mentioned earlier a high percentage of the errors were found in sentences of this type. Second, during any particular run of the package, the computer keeps track of those questions which have been answered correctly (Olmsted 1975:15). These will not be used again. However, a question answered incorrectly remains in the set of possible questions and may, or may not, occur again in that run of the package.

Many CALL packages do not have the sophistication of random questioning. It is certainly easier in programming terms to have a straightforward list of questions which the student works through in consecutive order. Such a package can be used once or perhaps twice, but after that it is unlikely to present any interest or challenge. Given the effort which has clearly been put into GERAD, particularly in terms of the initial explanation and the facility to refer to parts of the explanation as required, the producers intended it as a package to be used with profit on several occasions. However, if randomizing is too difficult, an alternative would be to have several lists of sentences within the program to be worked through in turn. A student could then specify a new list of examples on each occasion.

5.2.6 Ending the exercise

When the student has attempted ten questions the following message is printed:

Do you wish to continue?
Type C to continue or type Q to quit.

The student thus has the option to stop at this point, or to go on for another ten turns, at which point the option to stop will be given again. When the student decides to finish working on GERAD, the last score given is the final score, and there follows a message expressing the hope that the student has enjoyed using GERAD. This point offers a good opportunity for indicating the existence of other CALL programs, particularly any related to the one just used. Alternatively, complaints and suggestions can be requested. In addition to the invitation to stop after each ten turns, there is a way of leaving the package at any point if required.

5.3 Technical details

The purpose of this chapter is to present a CALL package as it appears to the learner. From this point of view the programming behind it may be of limited relevance. Nevertheless, for the benefit of the curious, basic information on the program is given in this section (see also Ahmad & Rogers 1979).

GERAD was originally written in FORTRAN (FORTRAN–IV, ANSI version). The program is modular in design: there are separate modules which take care of the display of the introductory material, the randomization of questions, the checking of answers and the scoring of points. The great advantage of this approach is that a particular module need be written only once and then it can be used in a range of different programs.

Indeed, the randomization, checking and scoring modules in GERAD were taken from previously written packages for students of Russian.

While the program was first written in FORTRAN, a later version was written in BASIC. In fact some parts of the program which deal with strings of characters were easier to write in BASIC. Versions could be produced in various other programming languages. Some author languages (see section 6.6) might allow the teacher to produce a comparable package – though not all: for some the randomization procedure is impossible. GERAD originally ran on a minicomputer, but the later version runs on a microcomputer. In one respect, it might be more successful on a micro, that is with regard to the characters found in the German but not in the English alphabet. It is often easier to display such characters using a microcomputer than on many terminals used with mainframes and minicomputers. Where non-standard characters are essential, as for example in Russian programs, there is a variety of solutions; the use of a microprocessor is described in Ahmad & Corbett (1981). The authors of GERAD felt it was not worth going to such lengths for a German program, as there are alternative acceptable spellings for the non-standard characters in the German alphabet. Thus, in the example used earlier in the chapter, the adjective normally spelt *fließend* can be spelt *fliessend*. However, several microcomputers allow the user to specify special characters, such as *ß*, or French *ç*, relatively easily (see section 8.5).

5.4   Taking stock

In reviewing GERAD, the first point which deserves emphasis is that it is aimed at a specific problem – something which students consider difficult and which has been shown to give rise to numerous errors. The program written to meet this need is fairly complex. In return for a considerable investment of time, the authors have a package which has several notable features. First, the explanatory part of the package is in a separate file, which means that the teacher can easily improve this section without affecting the main program. More importantly perhaps, the student has a reasonable degree of control over the session; the main positive feature here is the help facility, which allows the student to call for information to help with any of the questions. Besides putting questions at random, the program keeps track of correctly answered questions and does not repeat these during a session. The combination of these features means that the package can be used profitably on several occasions. The facilities listed are handled by different program modules and they can be used in the development of further packages.

From a different point of view, however, GERAD is extremely simple –

it is a quiz. The student is asked a series of questions, told if the answer is correct (and given the correct answer if necessary), provided with a score and offered help if required. The same approach could be used for a wide range of grammatical topics: the use of prepositions, choice of tense and so on. And these could be problems in English or Serbo-Croat: there is nothing specifically German about the construction of GERAD. Of course, to the learner, the package would appear to be very different. The explanation and comments would bear no similarity to those in GERAD. The form in which the questions are put might well be different but the basic pattern could remain the same. Thus, given a CALL package which works successfully, the main elements and structure of the program can then be used as a template to produce other packages to deal with quite different linguistic material.

In view of the fact that the structure of the package is that of a quiz, we are brought back to our earlier question: 'Would you tackle this problem in this way?' A quiz can be a straightforward test – a check that the learner has mastered something. GERAD is not a simple test of that type. Rather it is intended to help the learner of German to come to understand a particular problem. This suggests that whether or not you would choose to do it this way depends on your general view of language teaching.

GERAD represents a considerable investment in time. A viable package could have been developed with less effort – by omitting the help facility or the randomization of the sentences, for example. Equally, further facilities could be added. Incorrect answers could be trapped and error messages could be printed, as discussed earlier. Or the student could be given the option to practise only strong endings first, and then the weak endings, before tackling the full complexity of the problem (this would require random selection within defined groups of sentences). The individual teacher must decide how much effort a particular package is worth. One can develop two simple packages in the same time as a single complex one, and students may derive more benefit overall from a less sophisticated approach to two different problems. Alternatively, once a really good program has been produced it may well be possible to exchange a copy of it for a second program produced by another teacher. At a lower level, we saw that there is a range of choices which the author of a package must make, such as the number of times the learner can attempt a question. Here there is little difference in terms of effort in preparation; it is purely a matter of the teacher's judgement.

Our first question: 'Would you tackle this problem in this way?' can only be answered by the individual teacher. If, however, the answer is 'Let someone else tackle it', then our second question becomes more relevant: 'Would you buy it?' Of course, the points made earlier are still relevant, as the package must do what the teacher wants in terms of fitting into the course being run. It must be evaluated as carefully as any other new materials. But there are also some mundane but vital questions to be asked. The first question concerns portability. Programming languages differ from computer to computer: they have 'dialects' (see section 6.3.1) which often give rise to more serious problems than those caused by dialects in natural language. As was stressed in section 2.2.2, it is therefore essential to ensure that the package was designed to run on the computer which the students will be using. The second question concerns **resilience** or **robustness**. By accident or occasionally by design, learners will give inappropriate answers to questions. An insufficiently resilient program will not be able to deal with this situation and will stop ('crash' in computer jargon). This is serious since it disrupts the learner's session, and may even leave the system requiring commands which the student will not know before another package can be run. Consider the end section of GERAD:

> Do you wish to continue?
> Type C to continue or type Q to quit.

A student might read this instruction hurriedly and type 'yes', a response not directly catered for. However, this eventuality is catered for in GERAD: after any response other than C or Q the two lines above are repeated, and the package continues or ends according to what the student types next. Of course, to test resilience it is necessary to see the package running and, when trying it, make numerous incorrect responses both reasonable and unlikely.

5.5 Conclusion

We have considered a particular package which in its day had some novel features. While it is helpful to concentrate on a single package for purposes of exposition, this cannot do justice to the range of possible program types, which goes far beyond the tutorial mode represented by GERAD. These possibilities will be discussed in chapter 7. We have seen that the design of a CALL package presents numerous choices, some of which make the task of writing the package much more or much less difficult, others of which may make a considerable difference to the student but are largely irrelevant to the effort expended in writing the package. Thus all the main choices come back, where they belong, to the language teacher. While these decisions must be made primarily on pedagogical and linguistic grounds, familiarity with the computing implications is an advantage. For this reason, we take a closer look at the computing which lies behind CALL programs in chapter 6.

6 Computers, computer programming and programming languages

Throughout our discussion we have dealt mainly with the learner, and the learner's interaction with the computer. In the last chapter we concentrated on a specific CALL program as it appears to the learner. We now focus on the role of the teacher in CALL. Decisions about the role of the computer in the language-teaching curriculum are discussed in chapter 7. In this chapter we concentrate on the software aspects of CALL, expanding on some of the questions and concepts introduced in chapter 2. If it is to act as a vehicle for learning, the computer must be given linguistic data, and instructions on how to present these data to the student. Such instructions are called **computer programs**. Writing good CALL programs demands skill, imagination and time. Particularly for the latter reason, many teachers will not wish to write their own computer programs. Even so, a certain understanding of some of the general principles of how the computer works is useful.

Our consideration of computer programming will be in the context of the teacher and the instructions given to the computer to conduct a CALL session. We begin by describing briefly what computers do, and how the machine 'understands' a human being (section 6.1). Since the whole point of computer programming is the communication of instructions from man to machine, programming languages – the medium for the communication of these instructions – are an essential part of our discussion (sections 6.2 and 6.3). Language, whether a natural language or an artificial language like a programming language, requires a vocabulary and rules of grammar, which specify how the vocabulary items can be arranged into grammatical statements in the language. In section 6.4 we describe the general principles of the vocabulary and of the grammar ('syntax') of programming languages. In order to show how these items work in practice, a simple CALL program is presented in two standard programming languages (section 6.5) and this is followed by a review of higher-level author languages in section 6.6.

This chapter constitutes a brief introduction to a subject which is seen by many as shrouded in mystery. We hope to give non-specialists some indication of how computers, and computer programming in particular, work. Learning a programming language is a trivial matter when compared to the task of learning a natural language. There are many well-written textbooks and manuals on programming languages available to take the reader further.

6.1 A brief introduction to computers and computer programming

The computer, by definition, performs computations. In this section we discuss what these computations are, how the machine performs them, and how they relate to programming languages.

6.1.1 What can a computer do?

The computer receives data in the form of numbers and letters. It processes the data according to instructions from its human user(s), and provides the user with information as a result. These instructions, taken together, are the computer program. They are conveyed to the computer by means of a programming language. The word 'program' derives from the Greek work *programma*, meaning 'public notice, edict'. Computer programs are sets of clear and unambiguous instructions to the computer. They are imperative: they tell the computer what to do, and how to do it. **Data** are the raw material which is fed into the computer. The program instructs the computer what to do with the data, and how to present the result – the **information** – to the user. These three terms – data, program, and information – should be used with care.

A modern computer is essentially an arithmetic machine. It is consequently known as a 'digital computer'. All the data which it handles are in the form of numbers – even letters and punctuation marks are ultimately represented as numbers. Each letter, digit (i.e. numeral) and punctuation mark has a number of its own, following one of the standard international conventions like ASCII (the American Standard Code for Information Interchange). When the user presents the computer with data, whether it is in the form of words, letters, digits, spaces, or punctuation marks, the computer interprets these data as sequences of numbers. The word *cab*, for instance, is represented inside the computer by a sequence of three numbers in the ASCII code, 99–97–98. *CAB*, in capitals, is translated by the computer into 67–65–66. In this way the computer is able to distinguish the different letters and numbers as they are fed into it from the keyboard, tape or disc. Everything the computer then does with the data – additions, multiplications, checking words and letters, adding words and letters to the end of sentences, and so on – happens inside the computer as strings of numbers. The computer then obligingly re-translates all these internal numbers into ordinary characters (numbers and letters), so that the human user can easily understand the output – the information which the computer produces as the result of its program.

The number system which the computer uses is somewhat different from the one we are accustomed to. Our arithmetic, as a result of our having ten fingers, is decimal: we think and count in tens. It would be complicated to construct a machine which worked in tens. Instead, the computer uses the simple fact that any number can be translated into 'binary' code. In the decimal number 12 we know that there is 1 'ten' and 2 'units' (1 in the 'tens column' and 2 in the 'units column'), making a total of 12 units. The number 112 contains 1 'hundred' (= ten squared), 1 'ten', and 2 units. In binary notation, counting is done not in tens but in twos. Thus in binary notation, the form 10 contains 1 'two' and no units (1 in the 'twos column' and 0 in the 'units column') and stands for the 'ordinary' number 2. Binary 110 contains 1 'two-squared' (=4), 1 'two' and no units, making a total of 6 (4+2+0=6). The binary way of translating numbers is ideal for the computer, since the 0 can be translated as 'current off' and 1 as 'current on'. These are precisely the two states of electric circuits – the current is either off or on. Binary 110 is therefore like three circuits, with the current on, on and off respectively. As we have said, in 'normal' terms the word 'CAB' is represented by the (decimal) numbers 67–65–66. The computer would convert this into binary notation: 01000011–01000001–01000010. Thus eight bits (a byte) are used to store each character, as pointed out in section 2.1.1. It might seem a lot of trouble for the computer to have to handle such long strings of zeros and ones, but in fact it is much easier, and faster, than trying to manage decimal arithmetic.

6.1.2 The computer system

As we saw in chapter 2, the computer consists of several components. There are three main units: the input unit, the central processing unit (CPU), and the output unit. The input unit receives data from the external world via the input devices like the keyboard, tape, discs, and so on. The data are processed into information in the CPU and are passed on to the output unit, which communicates the processed data – the information – to the outside world via output devices like the VDU. The CPU is the heart of the computer operation, and itself contains three components: the control unit, the memory unit, and the arithmetic/logic unit (ALU). The control unit controls everything which happens in the computer system. The memory unit is used to store digits, which can represent data, instructions from the program, or information. And the arithmetic/logic unit is capable of performing all the four arithmetic operations (addition, subtraction, multiplication, division) as well as the logical operations of comparison. (Given two numbers, the ALU can determine which number is greater, or whether the numbers are equal.) The overall structure of the computer system, then, looks like the diagram in figure 2.

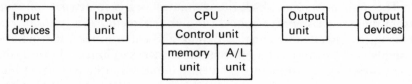

Figure 2 The components of a computer system

This basic design, which might look as if it were useful only for mathematics, can in fact handle all the different types of programming tasks and data involved in CALL, precisely because the numbers can stand for letters, punctuation and words as well as digits.

Typically, the data and instructions are brought into the memory unit from peripheral storage such as disc or cassette (see section 2.1.3). The memory unit is organized like a series of boxes, the so-called 'storage locations'. These boxes are numbered consecutively, like addresses on a street, and can contain data and instructions coded in bits. A program and its associated data are stored in the memory. The user then instructs the computer to start ('execute' or 'run') the program. The control unit fetches the instructions, and interprets them to determine what type of operation is to be performed on a given data item. The control unit then instructs the arithmetic/logic unit to perform the instruction, and either outputs the result to the user (for example, by displaying it on the VDU), or stores it in its memory for future use. The control unit then fetches the next instruction, and the whole cycle begins again. The memory where the instructions and data are usually stored is known as **random-access memory** or **RAM**. This type of memory can be constantly filled, erased when no longer required, and then refilled. It contrasts with ROM, which we will meet shortly in section 6.2.2.

The modern digital computer is, then, really a high-speed arithmetic machine. It can store and retrieve numbers in memory, it can perform arithmetic and logic operations on the numbers, and it can decode ('understand') instructions, again stored in the form of binary numbers. All these operations, together with input and output, are performed with great speed and accuracy. Since the instructions can be stored in the CPU memory unit, the computer – unlike a simple calculator – does not require step-by-step instructions. The computer, to use the original (c. 1940) name for such machines, is a 'stored program computer'. Incidentally, it is interesting to note that the first computer, ENIAC (1944), was called the 'Automatic Sequence Controlled Calculator', and the inventors were very proud of the fact that ENIAC was a 'stored program' machine. This helpful phrase was dropped in the early 1960s, leaving the simple term 'computer' in general use.

6.1.3 The discriminatory power of the computer

Another reason for the computer's power is its capacity for discrimination. We have mentioned above that data and instructions are both stored in the form of numbers, and the control unit fetches the (next) instruction from memory to begin each step in the program. Usually, of course, the instructions are stored at consecutive addresses (or storage locations), which means that they are fetched by the control unit in simple linear order. It is also possible to arrange a program so that it can 'jump' to another specified location in memory, so bypassing the next location in memory where instructions are stored. By making the machine jump backward a few steps, we can make it repeat an operation in the program any number of times. We can also program the machine so that this backwards 'jump' is conditional, and the program only jumps back if certain conditions are met. The GERAD package (discussed in chapter 5) gave a useful example of just this process of 'jumping back'. In GERAD the computer performs one set of instructions if the student's answer matches the specified 'correct' answer: it congratulates the student and awards one point before proceeding with the next question. If the student's answer is incorrect, the computer follows a different path: the student sees a message saying that the answer was wrong, offering hints, and suggesting that the question be taken again (the jump back in the program sequence). We can repeat this process until the student gives the correct answer, or until he or she has had a specified number of attempts at the question. If all the eventualities can be anticipated, and translated into instructions in the computer program, the programmer can use the computer's power of discrimination to take appropriate action for each of them. This discriminatory power distinguishes computers from other programmed machines like washing machines or dish-washers.

The computer's discriminatory power can also be seen at work in a typical CALL program which uses only a small number of instructions to display a number of questions, asking for answers for each question in turn. Depending on the student's answer, the program executes a given set of instructions. For each question the essential operations are the same: display the question, input the student's answer, check the student's answer, and respond to the student. The instructions need not be repeated in the program for each new question and student answer.

In machine terms, the same set of instructions can be used to process each different data item (the student's answer). The program must then be able to find the location in memory where the next question is stored, and so on. Furthermore, the computer can modify not only data, but also its instructions, and in so doing can achieve economies of scale. To take a simplified example, for a CALL program which has a vocabulary of five words, there is no need to write individual instructions to display each word, and to obtain the anticipated correct answer for each word. It is sufficient to tell the computer to modify the instruction so that it can fetch the questions and the associated answers. The easiest way to do this is to assign a number to each question and its associated right and wrong answers. This number might be called x, which is equal to 1 at the start of the program. The computer is told to get question x, display it to the student, check the student's response against the anticipated right and wrong answers (also numbered x), and to take appropriate action. The program is then told to add 1 to the value of x. x is now equal to 2. The program 'jumps back', repeating the same sequence, except that this time it is handling question number 2. This 'loop' can be repeated as many times as is necessary.

The power of the computer lies in its ability to perform arithmetic operations with speed and accuracy, to use its power of discrimination to analyse instructions and associated data, and to use the flexibility of the stored program to determine the sequence of operations to perform. These abilities depend on the computer's physical attributes, its hardware. This hardware is inert and can do nothing without a program. The effectiveness of the program depends on the ability of the human programmer to break down a complex task into a series of small, precise sub-tasks which can be translated into terms which the computer can 'understand', so that it can then perform the task. Indeed, it is the intuitive ability of a human being to analyse a given task and to use and blend in the various machine operations for executing the task which makes computers as widely used as they are. This (human) ability to analyse problems in terms of their constituent parts, to express them in a formal language, and to present them to the computer as a series of sub-tasks, is what realizes the versatility and power of the computer.

Programming languages belong to the less concrete aspect of the computer: the software. Programming languages are formal languages, like arithmetic, and as such they show no ambiguity (cf. section 4.2.1). This is achieved by having a restricted alphabet, vocabulary, and rules of grammar. There is no semantic vagueness, none of the allusiveness of natural language.

6.2 Programming languages

In order to illustrate a programming language, we begin by considering a simple problem of how we might instruct a machine to add two numbers, and store the result of the addition. For the sake of generality we shall not refer to any specific pair of numbers, but shall call these numbers (data items) A and B. The sum of the numbers will be represented by S. The 'formula' for the process of addition is quite simple:

S := A + B

which reads as 'add ('+') B to A and assign (':=') the result of the addition to the symbol S.

6.2.1 Low-level languages

For a computer, the formula above is not really quite so simple. Let us assume that the numbers which the symbols A and B represent are already stored in the computer's memory. In order to perform the addition, a typical machine has to be given four instructions to obtain S by adding A and B:

GET A	[from the memory]
GET B	[from the memory]
ADD A AND B	[in the arithmetic/logic unit]
STORE THE SUM S	[in the memory unit]

This program (or set of instructions) is written in mnemonics like GET, ADD, STORE, and each mnemonic represents some basic machine operation. Each operation refers to some data item, such as the symbols A, B and S, which contain numbers. The program is referred to as an **assembly-language** program. Furthermore, this program has to be stored somewhere in the computer's memory, which means that the address locations of the instructions must also be provided. In the previous section we said that the computer is essentially an arithmetic machine, since it can receive and operate only with numbers presented to it as binary digits. The machine on its own is incapable of understanding (or, more appropriately, interpreting) the operation codes like GET, ADD, STORE. For the machine to execute instructions like GET A, in the example above, the instruction itself must be in the form of digits. The designers of computer systems assign to each operation (arithmetic, logic, memory, jump, and so on) a unique number. If a programmer knows these codes, he or she can code the programs in terms of numbers, referring to the operation code, and to the memory location where the data are stored. This is known as **machine code**. For instance, the computer designer might set up the following table:

OPERATION	CODE
GET	01
STORE	10
ADD	11

(The numbers are, of course, in binary notation, for the reasons given above.) Suppose we have stored the data – the numbers contained in A and B – at memory location 1100 and 1101, and we wish to store the processed result(s) at location 1111. The assembly-language program earlier in this section translates into machine code as:

```
GET A      01 1100
GET B      01 1101
ADD        11
STORE S    10 1111
```

6.2.2 *High-level and low-level languages: a comparison*

Such machine-language programs are called 'low-level' programs. The term 'low-level' has no pejorative overtones. It simply means that at this level each detailed operation is spelt out precisely for the computer step by step. Machine code is the lowest-level language. Assembly is a low-level language, but it stands between machine code at the lowest level, and high-level languages, which contain statements like 'S: = A + B'. This last, in fact, is a statement in the high-level programming language PASCAL. Programmers using high-level languages do not have to specify details of the memory and other operations on individual brands of computers. They are more general, less specific. They refer directly not to operations which occur within the computer, but to processes more easily recognizable to human beings.

Computer manufacturers nowadays supply special-purpose programs to translate the program written in a high-level language into the low-level language of the computer on which the program is to be run. These special translation programs are called **compilers** or **interpreters**. They make it unnecessary for the user to worry about assembly language or machine code, which is handled automatically by the computer itself. The user is concerned only to provide an accurate, correct program written in a high-level language. Such a program can in principle be run on any machine which has a suitable interpreter to translate a high-level program into low-level language or code. The interpreter may be permanently stored in **read-only memory** or **ROM**. ROM allows what is stored there to be retrieved whenever required, but unlike RAM it does not allow the user to change or erase it.

6.3 High-level languages

The vocabulary and grammar of high-level programming languages are not tied to the operations of individual computers. Instead, they are more related to mathematical notation. A programmer is allowed to 'invent' new words for his or her own use, provided that these words are used in a systematic and disciplined way. These invented words usually refer to objects which the programmer wishes to manipulate in the course of the program, very much like the x's and y's of algebra. Computer programming languages, especially high-level languages, also have 'sentences' – sequences of instructions, which must be combined in clearly specified ways if the computer is to understand them and execute them properly. Each high-level language has a small vocabulary of words with precisely-defined meanings. With these tools, and working within these rules of syntax, the programmer can specify a variety of tasks for the computer to do.

6.3.1 *The evolution of programming languages*

It was the development of assembly languages – or rather languages which the machine itself can translate into machine code – which paved the way for high-level programming languages. The origins of high-level programming languages can be traced back to the **autocodes** of the early 1950s. These codes were sets of instructions which were orientated more towards the human user than towards the machine itself.

The autocodes were the forerunners of many high-level languages in use today, including FORTRAN (c. 1954), COBOL (1960) and ALGOL (1960). FORTRAN and ALGOL were adopted by the scientific communities of the United States and Europe respectively, and COBOL became the *de facto* standard of the business community, with a total investment in programming which is now in the region of $100 billion. Higman (1967:5) includes among the salient features of a 'good' programming language that it should: 'Take over without change as much as possible of any well-formed descriptive language which is already established in the field in which the problem originated.' As mathematics is the descriptive language of the physical and engineering sciences (the major users of FORTRAN and ALGOL), it is no coincidence that the grammars of FORTRAN (FORmula TRANslation language) and ALGOL (ALGOrithmic Language) are borrowed from mathematical notation rather than from natural language. COBOL (COmmon Business Oriented Language), on the other hand, borrows its vocabulary and grammar from certain parts of English, and there are specific provisions in the language to handle data typical of business and commercial activity like office records. To illustrate the differences between the three languages, we will rewrite the instruction in section 6.2 above to add two numbers (S:= A + B) in FORTRAN, ALGOL and COBOL:

```
FORTRAN:    S = A + B
ALGOL:      SUM := A + B;
COBOL:      ADD B TO A GIVING S
```

The early high-level languages were very much orientated towards particular subject domains. COBOL was not readily usable for problems in physics or engineering, while FORTRAN and ALGOL were less help for producing inventories, payrolls, invoices, and so on. This is not to say that these tasks were impossible in any of the other languages, rather that certain languages were inherently better adapted to certain types of problems. Later examples of high-level languages include LISP (LISt Processing language, c. 1960), BASIC (Beginners' All-Purpose Symbolic Instruction Code, c. 1964, see section 3.1.3), SNOBOL (c. 1964), PAS-CAL (c. 1970, named after the French philosopher-scientist Blaise Pascal), PROLOG (PROgramming in LOGic, c. 1974), C, and ADA. These languages are more suitable for general purpose use, and some are more readily available on smaller computer systems. We shall discuss BASIC and PASCAL shortly, since they are the most widely available languages on microcomputers.

6.3.2 Standards and dialects of programming languages

The translation programs (compilers or interpreters) which convert the instructions of the high-level language into the low-level language of the computer are supplied by the manufacturer, and comply with internationally recognized 'minimal standards'. These minimal standards define the 'minimal' vocabulary and grammar of each programming language. The standards of high-level languages are defined by organizations like the American National Standards Institution (ANSI), which has set the standards for BASIC, FORTRAN and COBOL, and the International Organization for Standardization (ISO), which has set the standards for PASCAL. Not all high-level languages are available on all computers because the manufacturers do not provide interpreters or compilers for them all on their computers. On smaller computers there are usually only two or three interpreters or compilers, and on microcomputers there is usually only an interpreter for BASIC. In general, BASIC and PASCAL appear to be the most widely available languages, followed by COBOL and FORTRAN. LISP and PROLOG are gaining currency.

Programming languages also undergo evolutionary changes. These changes result in part from genuine advances in computer science. There have been two major specification reports on the FORTRAN language (FORTRAN–66: 1966; FORTRAN–77: April 1977). Each version of FORTRAN is better than the previous one, allowing more facilities for programmers, and indeed progressing towards a higher-level programming language with each revision. FORTRAN–8x, which is already being designed for the late 1980s, will incorporate a more sophisticated level of abstraction for special user problems, and will take advantage of the developments in hardware. BASIC, although first released in 1964, was not standardized until 1978, when the American National Standards Institution released the 'minimal' BASIC standards. This standardization of the language followed a period of more than a decade, during which BASIC had undergone six major revisions at Dartmouth College alone (McGettrick 1980, 91–2). PASCAL was released in 1970 by the publication of the now famous PASCAL Report. This report was written by Jensen and Wirth, and is now available in the form of a textbook (Jensen & Wirth 1978).

Some changes, however, result form the fact that the minimal standards represent compromises, and manufacturers find it difficult to work within them. They therefore introduce extensions to languages to suit their machines and clients. Dialects also evolve with the invention of more and more devices which can be attached to the computer. These devices require special sets of commands to control them. Different peripheral devices, particularly for input and output, have given rise to Microsoft BASIC, APPLE–BASIC and 'hyphenated PASCAL', prefixed by the name of the university where it was developed: UCSD–PASCAL (University of California at San Diego), HULL–PASCAL, and so on. All these dialects conform to the minimum standards laid down by the international standardization bodies like ANSI and ISO. Each dialect, however, also has its own special additional words, commands and features. Sometimes these special features require special hardware, which means that the dialect can only be run on computers with precisely that hardware. The situation is very much like the regional dialects of a natural language: to understand the dialect fully, one must live in the region where it is spoken. APPLE–BASIC, for instance, extends the vocabulary and grammar of standard ANSI BASIC so that it is easier for programs written in BASIC to control speech-output devices, or special-purpose circuit boards to handle more than one script on the monitor, such as Roman and Cyrillic. BBC–BASIC has various useful extensions, including one for drawing line diagrams easily, even though such graphic programming is one of the hardest areas of general programming languages (see also section 8.5.1).

When buying programs written in high-level languages like BASIC and PASCAL, it is imperative that the buyer makes sure that the program is written in a dialect which his or her computer can 'understand': in other words, there must be an interpreter (or compiler) for precisely that variety of BASIC or PASCAL available for the user's computer. It is generally not advisable for the novice programmer to try to translate from one dialect into another. This task is notoriously full of pitfalls, and even experienced programmers avoid such translation tasks.

6.4 The vocabulary and grammar of a high-level programming language

Consider again the instruction for adding (any) two numbers together:

S := A + B

If we parse this instruction (or 'expression', or 'sentence'), or identify each constituent we obtain:

S	:=	A	+	B
name	operation	name	operation	name

In more general terms, we can re-phrase this as:

S	:=	A	+	B
noun	verb	noun	verb	noun

There are similarities and differences between the vocabularies of programming and natural languages. The two language types are similar in that the symbols in a programming language can be classified into nouns and verbs, just as in natural languages. The nouns S, A and B are names, and the verbs + and := are like imperatives: add two things together and store the result in S. However, the differences between programming and natural languages are more striking. Programming languages have simple syntax which is totally regular. Their vocabulary is small, often of the order of 100 or so words. Since the purpose of the programming language is to communicate unambiguous instructions to a computer, the symbols of the programming language are interpreted very rigidly.

6.4.1 The verbs of a programming language

High-level programming languages allow the human user to communicate data to the machine (via an input device) and the machine to communicate information back to the user (via an output device). This is done by commands similar to natural-language verbs. Input commands are usually INPUT or READ, and the output commands are PRINT or WRITE. For instance, if we wish to have the computer display the results of the addition instruction 'S:=A+B', we would construct the small program:

S := A + B
PRINT S

where 'PRINT S' is like a Verb + Noun construction: 'print the sum'. When this program is run, the value of S will be output on a suitable output device like a VDU or a printer. For the user it all looks simple. For the computer, the command 'PRINT S' is in fact equivalent to several machine operations including: obtain the value of S from memory, convert its value from binary code into decimal notation, and communicate this value of S to the output device, via the output unit. All this takes place inside the computer, in machine code, and the user need never be involved.

So far we have used A and B to denote any two numbers. If the program is to execute the instruction 'S:=A+B' we have to let the computer know what values A and B have. Say that the numbers we wish to add are 1 and 2. Then we must include the following lines in the program:

```
A := 1
B := 2
S := A + B
PRINT  S
```

In computer language, we 'assign' the value 1 to the variable A, and the value 2 to the variable B. S is also a variable, and takes on different values, depending on the values which we assign to A and B. In the example above, S has the value 3. If, however, we assigned the value 5 to A, S would have the value 7, and so on. Whenever we want to add a different pair of numbers, we will have to change part of the program. The instructions to assign values to A and B have to be changed every time a new pair of numbers is to be added. Programs are seldom written for such specific data as in our examples so far. Indeed, programs are almost invariably written in a more general fashion, so that they can be used for different data without the user having to change the actual program. Instead of assigning particular values to A and B within the program, we should save the program in computer memory with no specific values. We can then use the program many times, and each time we can assign different values to A and B by inputting numbers at a terminal. We can use the 'verb' INPUT to make the program obtain a value for A and B. When the instruction:

```
INPUT  A
```

is executed, the computer will indicate that it is ready to receive a number which it will assign to the variable A. Our new, more general program, then looks like this:

```
INPUT  A
INPUT  B
S := A + B
PRINT  S
```

This program can add any two numbers supplied by the user, and print the result, without requiring any changes to the program itself.

The output from this program, however, will appear rather curt: just one number in the corner of a VDU screen. For that matter, the input will be equally curt: the machine may display a question mark to prompt the user to type in a number – or it may simply wait for the user to type, without giving any other outward sign of life or interest. A verbal cue is now required. The computer must display a string of characters like 'Hello, give me a number', or 'The sum of the two numbers is ...'. The machine on its own cannot be so intelligent, so the computer must be instructed to prompt the user to type numbers. A short piece of text like:

Please give me a number.

will do. When the text string: 'Please give me a number.' is typed into a program, the text string must be enclosed within quotation marks, so that the computer knows that it is dealing with text, and not with a variable like A. For instance, the command:

PRINT "A"

will cause the computer to print the letter A on the screen. But the command:

PRINT A

will make it print the value of the variable A: 1, 2, or whatever the current value of A is. A is a variable, but "A" is a constant, which never changes its value: it is always the letter A. The values assigned to variables can be changed by the programmer, or can be changed by the computer during the running of a program.

So if we wish to display 'Please give me a number.', the instruction to computer will be (in BASIC):

PRINT "Please give me a number."

It is entirely up to the user what appears inside the quotation marks. If we want to say the same thing, but in German, the command to the computer would be:

PRINT "Gib mir eine Zahl, bitte."

And similarly for other languages. We can now rewrite our simple program to input two numbers, add them together, and print the sum. This time, however, there is a more clearly interactive character to the program, since we include the prompts and text from the computer:

```
PRINT  "Please give me a number."
INPUT  A
PRINT  "Please give me another number."
INPUT  B
S := A + B
PRINT  "The sum of the two numbers is"
PRINT  S
```

A single PRINT instruction can be used to display the value of more than one variable at a time. For instance, the program:

```
A := 1
B := 2
PRINT  A, B
```

when executed will display the values of the variables A and B. The sequence 'A,B' in the program is called a **data list**. Data lists can contain both variables and constants, provided that each item is separated from the next with a comma, and constants containing text (string constants) are surrounded by quotation marks. The program:

```
NAME:="Fred"
PRINT  "The man's name is ",NAME
```

will print on the screen the message:

The man's name is Fred

6.4.2   The nouns of a programming language

As we mentioned in the previous section, programming languages have two types of data items: variables and constants. The constant data type are like the proper nouns of a natural language. They always refer to the same thing, and cannot be changed. It makes no sense to write a program command like:

```
1 := 2
```

Constants cannot change their values, and programming languages do not allow such statements.

The variable data type, whose value can (or will) be changed during the execution of a program, are like the common nouns of a natural language. The noun 'car' can refer to a Ford, a Bugatti, or a Moskvich. Similarly, the variable A can be assigned the value 1:

```
A := 1
```

or we can extend the instruction:

A := A + 1

which has the effect of adding 1 to whatever value A has at the present time in the program. If we run both commands in order, A will end up having the value 2. The variable data type can be thought of as a container for a value, so that when we say that the value of the variable A is 1, what we really mean is that the value contained in the variable A is 1. Containers may be empty, and so may variables. An empty variable has a name (such as A) but no value, and is said to be 'undefined'.

Data items are of different types; the main types are numerical and non-numerical. In a certain sense, the type of a data item determines its meaning, and limits the uses to which it can be put in programs. The *numerical* data type is a sequence of digits forming a single numerical value (number). There are two main types of numbers: the *integer* type (whole numbers), and the *real* type (numbers with decimal places, like 3.14159). There are also two non-numerical data types. We have already met *string* (text, character) data types. There is another non-numerical data type called *Boolean*, after the nineteenth-century English logician George Boole. String data types contain letters. Boolean data types can have only two values, TRUE and FALSE. For CALL purposes, the string data type is of particular importance. One advantage of a classification of types of data is that it helps the user *not* to write meaningless programs for the computer. The computer's compiler (the translation program from high-level to low-level language) ensures that the types of data in a program are consistent with the operations that are to be performed on the data. You cannot divide philosophy by 3.456, any more than you can make 654 into a passive.

6.4.3 The conjunctions and other parts of speech of a programming language

One of the most important (logical) conjunctions used in programming languages is the conjunction IF, used together with the conjunction THEN (and in some cases with the adverb ELSE). Consider a simple CALL program, in which we are trying to match a student's response (which has the chosen variable name: SR) with a pre-stored correct answer (chosen variable name: CA). If the student has the correct answer, we want the program to print the message 'Your answer is correct.' The appropriate instruction is:

IF SR=CA THEN PRINT "Your answer is correct."

Note that this instruction is in effect a combination of two instructions. The first instruction checks whether the student's response (SR) is in fact the same as the stored correct answer (CA). If this is so, then, and only then, the computer will execute the other half of the program instruction, and print 'Your answer is correct' on the screen. It is also possible to write commands like:

IF SR=CA THEN PRINT "Your answer is correct."
ELSE PRINT "Your answer is incorrect."

This combines three commands in a single, clear, two-line command.

Some elements of high-level programming languages have no obvious counterparts in natural language. One of these is statement labels, which allow programmers to identify individual instructions (statements, or 'sentences' in a programming language) either by numbers or by names. In the BASIC programming language all statements in a program must be labelled with a number:

```
10   INPUT A
20   INPUT B
30   S = A + B
40   PRINT S
```

(Note that in line 30 we use '=' and not ':=', which is part of the rules for writing programs in BASIC.) The consecutive numbers 10–40 refer to the instruction numbers in the program, and also indicate the order in which the computer should execute the instructions. The choice of numerals is entirely at the discretion of the programmer, and the lines could have been numbers 1–4, 100–400, 101–104, and so on. The numbers have another function, too. In most programming languages there is a command GOTO, which is used with a label like a line number to instruct the program which is the next line to be executed. If we add to our program the statement:

```
50   GOTO 10
```

our program will never stop running, since each time we get to line 40, and the result is printed on the screen, line 50 will direct the program back to line 10, and the whole process will start again. This is how the program handles the 'jump back' which we discussed earlier.

6.4.4 The syntax of a programming language

The syntax of a programming language specifies the combinations of symbols (vocabulary items) which are allowed in the language. For instance, there could be restrictions on the type of names or symbols which can be used in variables. Most programming languages require that variable names always begin with a letter (otherwise the computer could conclude that it is dealing with some curious type of number). The maximum number of letters which can be used for the names of variables differs from language to language, and in some cases can vary with the dialect of the programming language. PASCAL allows variable names of any length, but the first character must be a letter. Variable names in some dialects of BASIC are restricted to only one or two characters, whereas in some other dialects of BASIC, variable names can be up to six or eight characters long, again with the restriction that the first character must be a letter. Furthermore, the string variables of BASIC are distinguished from the numeral variables by a suffix: A$ is a string variable, while A is a numerical variable.

As in natural languages, most 'sentences' in a programming language have at least one noun and a verb:

A := 1

can be parsed as:

NOUN   VERB   NOUN
A   :=   1

The expression on the right of the assignment (':=') can be quite complicated:

A := B + C $\star$ D/E + F (G + H) / K

Most programming languages, however, do not allow expressions like this on the left of the assignment, where it is normal to find only a variable name. The whole statement 'A:=1' means 'give the value 1 to the variable A'. Reversing the order of the statement is not allowed:

1 := A

since it makes no sense to give a value A to a constant 1.

Some constructions in programming languages are like constructions in natural languages. A command like:

PRINT A

is like a construction in English with Verb + Noun Object ('Print the value of A'). The use of conjunctions (IF, AND, etc.) is also reminiscent of natural languages, as we saw in the instruction:

IF SR = CA THEN PRINT "Your answer is correct."

Note that the rules of syntax in programming languages are simple, transparent, and allow no exceptions.

In concluding this discussion, it is worth noting that the computer scientists interested in the design and specification of programming languages are borrowing extensively from developments in linguistics (McGettrick 1980), and that linguists are developing the computational paradigm of natural languages (Winograd 1983:13).

6.5   A simple CALL program in BASIC and in PASCAL

We now present a simple CALL program in two high-level programming languages, BASIC and PASCAL. This program is used to test a student's knowledge of the German equivalent of the English word 'big'. The only 'correct' answer this program will accept is the German word 'gross'. The strategy of our simple CALL program is as follows. If the student's reply matches the character string 'gross' then we will display a congratulatory and good-bye message 'Well done and good-bye for now.' If the student's reply does not match 'gross', the program will first display the message 'Your answer is incorrect. Please try again', and then start from the beginning again, asking the question 'What is the German equivalent of the word 'big'?' The whole process is repeated until the student types the correct answer 'gross'. Section 6.5.1 shows this CALL program in BASIC and 6.5.2 does it in PASCAL. (Note that there is no difference between opening and closing quotation marks in these languages.)

6.5.1   The CALL program in BASIC

```
100   G$ = "gross"
110   PRINT "What is the German equivalent of 'big'?"
120   INPUT S$
130   IF S$ = G$ THEN GOTO 170
140   PRINT "Your answer is incorrect."
150   PRINT "Please try again."
160   GOTO 110
170   PRINT "Well done and good-bye for now."
180   STOP
190   END
```

The interesting part of this program is instruction 160, which sends the program back to line 110 to ask the question 'What is the German equivalent of 'big'?' until the student answers correctly (lines 120 and

130). The program will STOP only if the variable S\$ (the student's reply) matches the pre-stored correct answer (the variable G\$). G\$ and S\$ are chosen simply to make it easier to read the program listing. X\$ and Y\$ would work equally well. For a detailed account of the use of BASIC for CALL purposes, see Kenning & Kenning (1983).

6.5.2 The CALL program in PASCAL

PASCAL is a much more sophisticated language than BASIC, and the way in which the program is written helps the user to see the various segments of the program. The version given is written in UCSD–PASCAL, which is found on a range of microcomputers:

```
Program quiz (input,output);
Var German__word: string;
Var student__answer: string;
begin
     German__word:='gross';
     writeln ('What is the German equivalent of "big"?');
     readln (student__answer);
     while student__answer <> German__word do
     begin
          writeln ('Your answer is incorrect.');
          writeln ('Please try again.');
          readln (student__answer)
     end;
     writeln ('Well done and good-bye for now.')
end.
```

The PASCAL program may seem cryptic, like the BASIC program, but perhaps slightly less so. The PASCAL program contains two variable 'declarations', which state what variables are going to be used in the program (German__word, student__answer), and what type they are ('char', for character). The BASIC commands INPUT and PRINT have been replaced in the PASCAL program by 'readln' and 'writeln' (read line and write line). More important, the words 'begin', 'while', 'do' help to structure the program, and to keep the various steps under close control. Each 'begin' has its own 'end', which again helps to structure and punctuate the various parts of the program.

6.6 Author languages

Many teachers are daunted by the prospect of writing computer programs for CALL. While programming languages are much simpler than natural languages, they require us to think in a somewhat different way, and so take some time to learn. For this reason, some teachers never give CALL a serious trial. This is a pity, since there are two other ways to create CALL materials, without any need to learn a normal programming language at all. The key is the notion of **author language**, introduced in section 2.2.1. An author language is a scaled-down programming language which is much less powerful than a full programming language, and is designed to help the user give instructions to the computer more easily than is possible with a full programming language.

Well over a score of author languages have been developed for CAL (Barker & Singh 1982). Some of them have been designed to teach specific subjects, while others are suitable for general-purpose use. Among the earliest were IBM's COURSEWRITER and Control Data Corporation's TUTOR language, which is associated with the PLATO system. Among the most widely used is PILOT, a general author language which has interesting possibilities for CALL (Starkweather 1969; Burke 1983). An example of an author language designed specifically for language teachers is EXTOL (Kenning & Kenning 1981; 1982).

We can use the same example as above to show how an author language looks in practice. We are asking the student for the German equivalent of 'big'. This example is from the E/MU author language (Sussex 1983):

```
.QUESTION.
What is the German equivalent of 'big'?
.RIGHT.
gross
.TEXT.
Well done and good-bye for now.
.ELSE.
.TEXT.
Your answer is incorrect.
Please try again.
```

The 'words' or 'commands' of the author language (which the teacher types in along with the text) start with a full stop in the left-hand column, and end with a full stop. The text of the question follows the '.QUES-TION.' command. The '.RIGHT.' command specifies a right answer, 'gross', and then displays some text as a result ('Well done and good-bye for now.'). The '.ELSE.' command picks up all student responses which are not identical to 'gross' and displays the text 'Your answer is incorrect. Please try again.' The student is then automatically taken back to the original question. Note that the whole segment of lesson is much closer to ordinary English: variables, programming language syntax, and so on do not confuse the issue. The simple convention for the author-language commands, the full-stop marker, is easy to handle. All the rest is done by a special program which the teacher obtains complete and which should be of no further concern. This program takes what the teacher writes in the author language (such as the material above) and presents the appropriate parts to the student.

An even easier introduction to authoring in CAL is provided by **authoring packages** (or **authoring systems**). Here the teacher does not even have to learn the words and rules of an author language. Instead, the authoring package displays menus; these are lists of choices, available to the teacher at each point in the lesson. The teacher chooses the option required, and the computer handles all the rest, prompting the teacher for the appropriate information at each stage. A menu in AUTHOR, an authoring package associated with E/MU, looks like this:

AUTHOR MENU
At this point in the lesson, you may:
1. display a screen of text
2. display a screen of graphics
3. start a drill
4. conduct a tutorial
5. assess the lesson so far
6. end the lesson.
Type the number of the option you need:

If option 3 is chosen, the program will go through a whole sequence of steps for setting up a drill, giving a prompt at each step for the appropriate instruction or linguistic data. The authoring package then creates the CALL program itself.

Authoring packages may work in conjunction with author languages. This means that the authoring package writes the program using author-language commands. The program then looks like one produced by a teacher using an author language directly. It might appear that there is no justification for including an author language in this system. Why not have the authoring package write programs directly in BASIC or PAS-CAL? Going through an author language has two advantages. First, it is easier. An authoring package which produces accurate BASIC or PAS-CAL is very difficult to write. And second, if the teacher makes an error in the lesson, and wants to make a correction, it is difficult to make any changes in BASIC, PASCAL or FORTRAN programs without a good knowledge of these programming languages. The author language, with its much simpler structure and less complicated rules of use, is much easier to manage when corrections are being made. A further advantage of the author-language approach is that the teacher can graduate easily from the authoring package to using the author language directly.

Authoring packages may, however, perfectly well omit the author-language component. One such is GAPFIL, developed by Michael Carr (University of East Anglia). This package allows the teacher to produce a range of gap-filling exercises. Another package is TES/T, written by Rex Last (Dundee University). Both packages were designed to run on micro-computers and are being made available commercially.

The drawback with both author languages and authoring packages is that they are, by definition, less powerful than normal programming languages. This means that they tend to restrict the teacher's scope and flexibility in creating CALL materials. Authoring packages tend to be most restricted in this respect. The restrictions are a trade-off against the ease of use, particularly for the beginner. Author languages, if well-designed, can allow the user access to certain aspects of the driver programs, especially the variables, which means that the teacher is not limited to the facilities offered by the terms of the author language itself. In this way the teacher can use the normal programming language in the driver program, and so enhance the CALL materials. There comes a point, however, where both the authoring package and the author language do not provide sufficient scope for the ambitious or imaginative teacher. At this point the teacher would be well advised to learn a fully fledged programming language, in order to be able to control the whole authoring process.

6.7   Conclusion

In this chapter we have outlined how a computer can be instructed to carry out a fully specified task. A programmer breaks down a given task into arithmetic, logic and memory operations which the computer can understand and act on. If these instructions refer directly to the fundamental operations of the machine, they are in low-level languages like assembly language or machine code. If, however, the instructions are more sophisticated, and allow the programmer to write the instructions in a more abstract manner, then they belong to a high-level programming language.

The computer is an arithmetic machine, and it deals with numbers in its internal workings. This does not mean, however, that the user has to turn all computer tasks into numbers before feeding them into the computer. On the contrary, the computer is very efficient at carrying out translations of this kind, so that it can turn the input into numbers, and then turn the numbers back into letters and so on, for the output to the user. In general, the computer carries out small-scale tasks of an arithmetical nature at very high speed. The feature which makes it more than just a calculator is its ability to combine thousands of such small operations into a program and to store this program.

Instructions are given to the computer in a programming language. The mathematical symbolism used in programming languages is due to a mixture of convenience and historical accident. Computers were first used by scientists, engineers and accountants; their influence, as well as their conceptual and theoretical orientation, was responsible for the bias of the uses to which the computer has been put, and the way it handles data and information.

There will probably never be a programming language which can cope fully with the complexities of natural languages. For the language teacher, computer languages are a 'step down'. Yet they can be of great interest, both for the comparisions they provide with natural languages and for their ability, however imperfect, to model such languages and to serve as a vehicle for CALL materials. So while the language teacher need not get involved in programming languages, to do so can be fascinating as well as useful.

7 The scope of the computer in language teaching

In this chapter we shall describe in some detail where and how in the language-teaching programme CALL can be appropriate and useful. Earlier we stressed that CALL cannot possibly cover the whole language-teaching curriculum, nor is it a self-contained methodology. This warning is timely. Educational technologies have in the past often been presented as easy solutions to large-scale problems. This means that many teachers – including many language teachers – are now suspicious of new technologies. Nonetheless, it would be premature to dismiss CALL from a feeling of distrust and cynicism born of previous disappointments. Rather, we must select those areas where CALL can contribute most successfully. Below we match some of the common language-teaching exercises and activities (section 7.1) with the capabilities of the computer, and extend this to include activities which the computer can add to this stock (section 7.2). After discussing the possibilty of monitoring student performance and CALL packages (section 7.3), we go on to consider how CALL can be integrated into the curriculum (section 7.4). Finally, we examine evidence on the important question of evaluation (section 7.5).

7.1 Activities in the language-teaching classroom

Wilkins (1974:ix) emphasizes that language teaching is a 'pragmatic' business, by which he means 'what works is good; what does not work is bad', although he concedes that evaluation is not an easy task. In this section, we discuss some of the activities which take place in the language-teaching classroom with a view to establishing which of these might be carried out using the computer, and which are best left to other means – at least for the present.

The question of evaluation, of deciding which activities attain which objective, is a difficult one. In devising a language-teaching programme, the teacher must have a clear idea of the objectives, and the course should then be tailored accordingly. A service course for Japanese chemists interested in reading specialist literature in English will be constructed very differently from an evening course in survival Spanish for British tourists to the Costa del Sol. Different exercises and activities will be needed in each case. This much is accepted nowadays without discussion.

However, exactly which activities or techniques are best suited to attain the stated objectives remains a subject of much controversy. The debate about the role of grammar in language teaching still continues, although it has shifted its ground somewhat in recent years. There is now general agreement that learning grammatical paradigms will not guarantee a facility in communicative skills. However, the place of grammar in the language-teaching curriculum is still disputed between the not necessarily exclusive camps of 'accuracy' and 'communicative competence' (cf. section 4.3). This debate cannot be resolved here. What we offer below is an outline of some of the more common activities found in the language-teaching classroom. We make no value judgements about their status as teaching techniques, aids to learning, testing techniques, or as objectives in themselves. Neither do we assess their suitability for particular types of course. This is a decision for the individual teacher in his or her own particular circumstances. There are a number of difficulties involved in setting up a typology of exercises of the more traditional kind (although Dodson 1967:178–80 has attempted this in some detail), since the exercises are a mixture of activities which practise discrete points of grammar, more global grammatical skills in various structural contexts, rule-learning techniques, techniques which can be adapted to a range of activities (e.g. multiple-choice), and some more 'real' items such as message taking/giving, writing letters and so on. The following list is representative but not exhaustive.

cloze exercises
comprehension exercises (aural or written, questions in mother tongue
    or foreign language)
dialogue (routine exchanges, role play, task-orientated, free)
dictation
gap-filling exercises
    e.g. affixes (prefixes, inflectional endings etc.)
        word/phrase in sentence
grammatical manipulation
    e.g. change the mood of a sentence
        combine two clauses into one sentence (by subordination,
            nominalization, etc.)
        change word class (verb into noun or adjective)
        change the voice of a sentence, change the tense, person or
            mood of a verb phrase
        give answers to questions designed to elicit particular structures
group/pair work
    e.g. dialogues, games
message production (memos, telegrams, notes, letters)
monologue presentation (tell or retell story, present argument)

multiple-choice exercises (answers presented in foreign language or
     mother tongue)
precis (various combinations for source text and precis in foreign
     language and mother tongue)
pronunciation and intonation (imitating sounds, words, phrases,
     sentences, reading aloud)
rule learning (explicit exposition - induction, rule discovery -
     deduction)
substitution exercises (lexical, grammatical)
translation (into or from foreign language at word, phrase, sentence
     or text level)
vocabulary work
     e.g. supply definition of given word or phrase in foreign language
                 or mother tongue
           supply a word or phrase from a definition in foreign language
           supply synonym or antonym
written composition (guided, free)

In addition to the more traditional exercises listed here, there are also the
more recently developed communicatively-based activities. The objectives of communicatively-based syllabuses are defined in terms of the uses
to which language is put in context. These are usually expressed in
'notional/functional' categories (see section 4.3.1). There are now a number of good publications available on the subject (Wilkins 1976; Munby
1978; Widdowson 1978; Brumfit & Johnson 1979; Van Ek & Alexander
1980; Littlewood 1981; Johnson 1982; Brumfit 1984).

  What is the potential for CALL with respect to these various activities?
One barrier to the use of the computer in communicatively-based exercises is the fact that it is easier to program the computer as a binary
machine; this often results in an uncompromising right/wrong approach.
As more recent developments have shown, however, the right/wrong
answer pattern can be used fruitfully in many other areas, where the
computer will actually expand the range of exercises available to the
language learner and teacher. Some examples are discussed in section 7.2.
We should not regard the use of the computer in a negative way because of
the things it cannot do as well as human beings. Instead we should
concentrate on some new things which it can offer, or even on some old
things to which it can give a new lease of life if used imaginatively.

7.2 Areas of language teaching suited to CALL

The closer the exercise approaches 'real' language activity, the greater will
be the synthesis of all the discrete skills mentioned in section 7.1. While

computers may be superior to human beings in the speed with which they can process data and in the amount of data which can be stored and reliably retrieved, they cannot compete with human beings in the processing of natural language (see section 4.2). It follows that completely free or uncontrolled exercises involving a synthesis of many different aspects of language are beyond the computer's scope. However, the newcomer to CALL should not assume that the lessons will be confined to narrowly conceived grammatical exercises. Below we consider these questions in greater detail.

7.2.1 Limiting factors

It is clear that the range of exercises and activities which can be performed in CALL is limited (and in some cases extended, see section 7.2.4) by the present stage of development in computer hardware and software. Let us first discuss the limitations imposed by hardware. Traditionally, language skills have been divided along two dimensions: written/spoken and receptive/productive. This produces four activities: reading, writing, listening and speaking. While these divisions are an oversimplification, since in real language activity it is often hard to separate one skill from another, it is nevertheless a framework which enables us to see in broad terms where the computer's present capabilities lie (see figure 3).

	production	reception
written	YES (writing)	YES (reading)
spoken	NO (speaking)	YES (listening)

Figure 3 Learner's skills which can be practised in CALL

It is an essential characteristic of natural language that it is primarily a spoken medium. This is obviously a problem for the computer since its ability to deal with speech is far less developed than its ability to deal with written signals (see section 4.4.2). The type of activities which are clearly not suited to CALL at present are those which require spoken production, such as spoken dialogue, oral summaries or answering of questions, and reading aloud. To be more precise, no exercise is possible which requires the computer to 'understand' or interpret the spoken input from the learner. CALL programs do exist where the learner is required to speak, but the computer cannot check or respond to this speech. Neither can the learner match response against model by replaying the tape as in the language laboratory. In this respect the computer is at present more like cassette-based courses for self-instruction (Roberts 1983:66). Nevertheless, the student can still practise certain listening skills, such as dictation, through this facility (see section 7.2.2). However, not all language courses aim to teach spoken skills (the course for Japanese chemists, for instance). Furthermore, many teachers use written activities either as a general approach, or as an end in itself. This all depends on the particular group of learners concerned. It may well be the case that 'writing' on the computer will assume new attractive dimensions for the learner whose motivation in this area was previously low (Papert 1980:30–1).

While low-cost computer hardware at present limits CALL primarily to the written language, other limitations derive from the present state of development in computer software. The kind of difficulties we have in mind are those outlined in section 4.2, which derive from the complex nature of natural language. (Of course, the processing of spoken language would encounter the same difficulties as the processing of written language. However, as we have pointed out, computer hardware still only allows limited speech recognition, or matching. Processing, or understanding, is a step further on.) We indicated in section 4.4.2 that CALL packages as they stand at the moment are still very literal-minded in their handling of student responses, though there are techniques for improving this, such as fuzzy matching and pattern markup (see section 5.2.3). Nevertheless, it is important to stress that what the computer is doing is matching, not understanding. A different problem arises with questions which have no specific right or wrong answer. In a comprehension exercise, for example, there may be a right answer in terms of a message, but several alternative structures to express that message. Other exercises which come into this category, and so pose difficulties for CALL, are precis writing, message production (memos, telegrams, notes, letters), composition (guided and free) and retelling a story, and supplying a definition.

In some of its forms, translation – one of the most controversial classroom activities in language teaching – is also a problem area for CALL. Translation can be used in the classroom in a variety of ways. Single-word translation is used as a means of explaining or testing meaning. Translation of sentences is used as a means of contrasting structures. However, translation of continuous text (often not distinguished in its nature from translation of isolated sentences) has been assigned many roles. These range from a means of practising the foreign language by translating from the mother tongue, to translating into the mother tongue as a professional skill.

Any CALL program which is based on translation, either into or out of the foreign language, will run into trouble if the answer is entirely in the control of the learner. These difficulties will increase as the exercise moves from translation of individual words or phrases to translation of continuous text. Exercises with translation of individual words or phrases will suffer from a lack of context, as in these English–German examples:

'view':	'Ansicht',	'Aussicht',	'Meinung';
	(opinion)	(view as from window)	(opinion)
'we stay':	'wir uebernachten';	'wir bleiben'.	
	(spend the night)	(remain)	

Exercises where only one correct answer is accepted for the translation of a sentence can be too prescriptive and restrictive, except for very limited applications. Consider the case where the target English translation of a sentence is: 'If I were rich, I would buy you a car.' A student might well produce the answer: 'If I were *a rich man*, I would buy you a car' or 'If I was rich, I'd buy you a car' and be marked incorrect.

Of course, it is possible to create CALL programs with a lot of data indicating alternative answers. This approach can handle many problems at levels *below* the sentence: that is, for letters, morphemes, words, and even phrases. But as the length of the answer grows, so too the number of possible different answers. Curtin *et al.* (1972) discovered some important limitations on CALL exercises which work at sentence level. And beyond the level of the sentence the difficulties multiply. In continuous text certain rules – like cohesion, choice of sentence focus, pronominal reference, and sequence of tenses – operate across sentence boundaries. To follow through such decisions from sentence to sentence is a highly complex task. Farrington (1981) has attempted such a program, called TEACHER, which consists of exercises in computer-based French prose composition. Each question put to the student has up to twenty answers stored. There are also devices for linking in sequence particular questions and answers. But handling such larger stretches of text requires not only imagination and ingenuity, but also a lot of hard work. Farrington's program serves to prepare the student to translate the passage; the translation is then done in the usual written form and marked by the teacher. The teacher must decide whether the benefits of a CALL program such as this are in proportion to the time invested.

7.2.2 Straightforward applications

While there are clear areas where CALL is not useful or poses significant problems, certain other activities can be dealt with efficiently. In this section we describe a representative sample of some of the more obvious and accessible areas of CALL. Inflexional morphology is one of the most obvious areas, since alternative answers are not usually possible. In such exercises the learner is required to provide noun endings, adjective endings or different parts of the verb, to change the grammatical case or the word order, and so on. These exercises may be be presented in different ways, for instance, gap-filling or changing a given form. But they are always concerned with discrete grammatical items. Exercises in derivational morphology, such as changing the word class of a given word, also fit easily into the single answer mould. Some of the methods used to present drills of this kind on the computer are discussed by Davies (1982).

Cloze exercises also present few problems for transfer to the computer since alternative answers do not often occur. While originally intended as a language test, cloze has come to be used more widely. It requires that the learner assess linguistic possibilities in the context of a text; this is certainly a useful skill to develop. The usual deletion interval is about every seven words, but in a CALL program the learner can be given a choice in order to adjust the level of difficulty, although decreasing the deletion interval will increase the possibility of alternative answers. The cloze technique is already in use as an authoring package for reading skills in English, French and German, and as a straightforward exercise (Davies 1982:62). In a more radical kind of cloze exercise, the learner starts with a screen blank except for punctuation marks. The task is to divine the text by 'buying' letters and guessing words (e.g. Johns's TEXTBAG). A familiar text might be best suited to this type of exercise or, alternatively, the text can be displayed to the learner at the beginning of the exercise as in Higgins's STORYBOARD. A version of this is now commercially available as an authoring package called COPYWRITE.

As well as gap-filling exercises and morphological manipulations, grammatical manipulations where there is a clear grammatical goal are also well suited to CALL. For instance, combining two clauses by subordination:

Jochen war traurig. Seine Mutter war krank. (weil)
(Jochen was sad.   His mother was ill.   (because))
Jochen war traurig, weil seine Mutter krank war.

Our example is taken from German, and indeed German subordinate clauses are beloved of program authors, since they provide the opportunity to show off the facility for moving words around the screen. However, such an exercise, as it is presented here, has the disadvantage of requiring a lot of typing on the part of the learner (see section 4.4.1). Other more serious objections also arise when it becomes apparent that there are more alternatives than were originally envisaged. Consider this example:

John arrived late. He missed the bus. (because)

There are a number of possible answers:

John arrived late because he missed the bus.
Because he missed the bus, John arrived late.
Because John missed the bus, he arrived late.
John missed the bus because he arrived late.

It is always advisable to have a test run of new programs with guinea-pig students or colleagues, since the program author may have difficulty in spotting alternative answers.

CALL may also be used in vocabulary work. Students can be asked to choose between alternatives as definitions of a given word (Davies 1982:11), although asking the student to supply a definition for a given word is too unrestricted as a CALL exercise. Supplying a word from a definition is also a clear possibility, since there is usually only one answer. Such an exercise can be presented in the form of a guessing game: 'What's white and woolly and eats grass?' Successive wrong guesses can be countered with the chance of further clues. This can be followed up in the classroom by learners producing written or oral definitions for the teacher or other members of the class.

Supplying synonyms or antonyms can be dealt with very neatly by requiring learners to match items from lists of words. Alternatively, simply typing in the answer is also possible, although this quickly becomes problematic if words are not contextualized ('old':'young' or 'old': 'new'). The matching can be done like a game of 'Snap' as in a package of that name produced by Jones (Roberts 1983).

Finally, there is one clear application for CALL using speech output: dictation. Although this is now being phased out in some public examinations, some teachers still prefer to retain it as an activity in their repertoire, especially for a language like English, where spelling can be a problem. Last (forthcoming b) describes a pilot version of a program which will enable teachers to set up computer-controlled dictation exercises using a BBC Model B computer linked to a cassette-recorder (see section 8.4 for consideration of technical possibilities).

7.2.3 Dealing with problems

So far we have outlined some areas of activity where the computer clearly does have a role to play, as well as some areas where it is not recommended. It is clear that some of the activities judged problematic for CALL are made more feasible by using flexible matching techniques (see section 5.2.3). A further alternative is to restrict the learner's choice through the presentation of limited alternatives. The use of multiple-choice format for comprehension exercises will be familiar to all teachers. So will its application to other areas in the lexical and grammatical domains. There is little point in describing such well-trodden ground here. We have already mentioned the use of multiple-choice in vocabulary work (section 7.2.2); in this section we show how the multiple-choice format can be used on the computer in quite different types of exercise.

The purpose of the first package is to show how a single function (for example, refusing an invitation) can be performed with varying degrees of politeness:

> Read the following conversation between Victoria and Albert. Albert would like to go out with Victoria.
>
> A: Hi! How's it going?
> V: Oh, not so bad. What about you?
> A: Er ... fine, thanks. But you're looking a bit fed up. Anything wrong?
> V: Not really ... just a bit bored.
> A: Well, perhaps... Maybe you'd like to see a film or something. How about tonight?
>
> What do *you* think Victoria's reply is? Choose one of the following, assuming that she wants to refuse firmly but without offending him:
>
> 1. Oh, thanks, but I'd really rather not.
> 2. Not with you I wouldn't!
> 3. Would you mind very much if I said 'no'?
> 4. Get lost!

Whichever alternative is chosen, an explanation of the stylistic effect of each response appears on the screen to explain the effect achieved. So (1) will be described as polite and a little shy, but nevertheless rather direct. (2) is offensive, poor Albert has no chance here; and so on. Such a program format can easily be used with different data. The written output on the VDU screen could also be accompanied by speech output. A program in a similar sociolinguistic vein (making requests), called LOAN, has been developed by Johns (1983:96), using a 'generative' technique (see section 7.2.4).

Another possibility for adapting the multiple-choice format is the traditional 'direction giving/understanding' exercise ('Could you tell me the quickest way to get to ...'). The learner is presented with a map to memorize with more or fewer features, according to the degree of difficulty chosen. In response to a question from the computer about the best way to get to X, the learner is given a number of alternative answers. The answer selected by the learner is then shown visually on the map (for example, using a flashing line) as well as in writing underneath. Wrong answers can be treated with some humour. ('Thanks a lot. I didn't really want to end up in the river.') The roles can be reversed so that the learner has to judge whether the computer is telling lies when asked for directions. Again, this can be accompanied by speech output.

These examples demonstrate that certain open-ended exercises can be tailored to meet the constraints imposed by the computer. Once this is achieved, it becomes apparent that such constraints can have interesting effects.

7.2.4 Expanding the range

Finally, there remain those activities indicated briefly in section 4.4.3, where the computer enables us to add to the stock of exercises available to the language teacher. Using the computer as a tool for language research, for stylistic or grammatical analysis, is discussed elsewhere (section 8.2). Here we shall consider just a few of the many other possibilities currently offered by the computer.

We pointed out in chapter 4 that many CALL programs can be presented to the learner in the form of a game. Computer games are now a feature of teenagers' lives, and vary from the very simple to the extremely complex. The educational value of many of them is not clear, apart from training abilities in co-ordination and shooting. However, there are many traditional games which can be adapted for language-teaching purposes. Probably the best known is Hangman, where students have to guess the letters in a word before their errors complete the drawing of a man on a gibbet. Particular games work more or less well in different languages. Though Hangman, for example, is successful in English, it is much less successful in a language like Italian. Various old games like Hammurabi and the Towers of Hanoi already exist in computer form. Such games introduce an element of competition and diversity. They are, as any teacher knows, a useful part of educational methodology. Many games can be adapted for CALL purposes by supplying language stimuli. Some of them, like Adventure, can be used to develop a wide variety of language skills, such as reading comprehension, vocabulary learning, expressing conditions and giving instructions.

Johns (University of Birmingham) has adopted a game format for many of his programs following what he calls a 'generative approach' to CALL which 'entails that no tasks are written in advance: what the computer program consists of is a series of instructions allowing the machine to create such tasks on the basis of its moment-by-moment interaction with the student' (Johns 1983:90). He emphasizes the active role of the learner as an intelligent guesser. His S-ENDING program is designed to act as a stimulus to classroom discussion of grammatical rules. The students challenge the computer's ability to give the correct form of words with an 's' ending (cat > cats; marry > marries). Group discussion involves formulating hypotheses about the rules the computer is using and then testing them out, particularly with a view to out-manoeuvering the computer with rare examples. Such a problem-solving approach is certainly possible as a normal classroom technique with a teacher's supervision. However, the teacher may not always be so regularly and thoroughly systematic in response to test-examples. Johns admits that while one of the main problems in devising such a program is working out the linguistic rules, the computer cannot fail to spot the weaknesses in suggested hypotheses once these are established.

Simulation exercises are a well-known application for computers in many subjects, such as economics and mathematics. They are becoming more popular now also in non-numerically based subjects such as geography and history. Simulations involve changing particular variables in a given situation to test the outcome. In CALL, 'simulation' has two possible interpretations. The first refers to games which simulate a 'real' environment. This is the way in which simulation has generally been understood in language teaching. Higgins's 'non-tutorial interactive' program MURDER is broadly of this kind (Higgins 1982). This sort of CALL program exploits the same principle as many of the communicatively-based activities now practised in the language-teaching classroom, but already suggested in 1974 by Littlewood (1974b:41). Programs which contain no actual language stimuli may also be used, although in quite a different way. For instance, Harrison's TOWN PLANNING program allows students to mark on a map of the town 'features such as one-way streets, zebra-crossings and so on, so that they can study the effects of their decisions on traffic and pedestrian flow' (Harrison 1983:86). Such programs may be used as a stimulus to discussion in the target language by small groups of learners who must decide on which course of action to take at each stage of the exercise. In coming to decisions, or evaluating their actions, the members of the group will need to use many different language functions, such as warning, persuading, asking questions, expressing conditions, admonishing and so on.

The second interpretation of the term simulation in CALL adds a new dimension to language exercises. The ability of the computer to manipulate data in order to test the outcome of decisions can be exploited using linguistic data. An example of this is Sharples's 'relative' command in his text transforming program WALTER (Sharples 1983:53–4) designed for use by primary-school children. Suppose the child types in:

Once there was a pretty princess. The princess lived in a big castle in a forest. The forest was dark.

The next step is to type in the command 'relative'. The text will then appear on the screen in the following form:

Once there was a pretty princess who lived in a big castle in a dark forest.

Sharples's motivation was to improve children's writing skills by allowing them to experiment with language using 'intelligent' word-processing techniques. Such techniques could be equally valuable in advanced language teaching or in linguistics in relation, for instance, to text or discourse structure. Ideas which could be pursued in this exploratory vein include swapping passives for actives in English, placing all Subject NPs at the beginning of main clauses in German, and so on. However, the 'intelligent' word-processing facilities needed to perform these operations require complex linguistic and computing knowledge, so they remain to date largely an area of interest rather than practice.

Another non-tutorial program type, although of a quite different kind, provides information as requested by the learner. An interesting version of this 'oracle'-type program is FORMAD, a program which has information on forms of address in Russian. The student can see this information if desired. Then the machine asks a series of questions, concerning a setting imagined by the user, about the status of the person addressed, the relationship between them, and so on. It then supplies the appropriate pronoun (polite or familiar) or title of address. An interesting point is that what the user learns is not so much the particular form given. The purpose of the exercise is rather in the computer's questions. The user learns the factors which are significant in the choice of forms of address. It is also worth noting that the program was written by a student at the University of Surrey (Antony Rummery) on the basis of class work. The advantages of having students involved in the production of CALL materials are considerable.

A number of programs take advantage of the computer's capacity to generate a large number of sentences from a simple set of rules and some data. Adjustments to the grammar and/or the lexicon can be tested for effect, or the learner might be asked to judge given sentences for accuracy. SYNTAX, another Russian program produced at the University of Surrey, generates 4320 sentences from a repertoire of sixteen words. The student is shown sentences at random and is asked to assess them, and to correct them when necessary. Semantic judgements might also be required or the learner could be asked to add to the data to test how this interacts with the rules.

Heuristic programs (ones that 'learn' as they go along) also have interesting possibilities for CALL. GETRAENKE is a game also developed at Surrey (Ahmad & Rogers 1981) where the learner plays a guessing game with the computer. The computer's task is to guess which drink the learner is thinking of. The game is of the kind: 'Think of a drink and I (the computer) will guess what it is.' Mind-reading is fortunately not yet a feature of computers. The game proceeds by a series of binary choices presented to the learner in the form of questions: 'Is it alcoholic?' 'Is it coloured?' The program will eventually reach a terminal node (the end of one possible path through the tree structure), for example 'gin' (see figure 4).

Figure 4   A possible path through GETRAENKE tree structure

It will then ask if 'gin' is the drink the learner thought of. If this is incorrect – if the drink was 'vodka' – the learner is asked to supply a question which distinguishes between 'gin' and 'vodka'. Such a question could be: 'Does the drink come from Russia?' (answer for vodka: 'yes'). The computer has then increased its store of drinks by one, and is suitably 'grateful' to the learner. A similar game, called SEEK, is discussed elsewhere for use with children in English mother-tongue work (Coupland 1983; Stewart 1983). Again the teacher must check that the game will work in the target language; it is difficult in Russian, for example, as the computer would be required to identify the declension of the noun supplied by the student in order to change the case ending correctly, according to the grammatical context. Many of the games produced in CALL are in fact based on well-established computer games such as those documented in Ahl (1973) and Krutch (1981). For a review of some interesting uses of the computer in non-tutorial mode, the reader can refer to Higgins (1983).

7.3 Monitoring

In section 7.2 we outlined some of the ways in which the computer can be of use in certain language-learning contexts. We now consider how the computer can be of direct benefit to the teacher by storing information about the student's progress through CALL programs, particularly those of an exercise format which give a score. It is possible, if desired, for a whole range of data about the student's presence and progress, about the CALL package itself, and other data to be reported back to the teacher, either on the VDU screen or in hard copy. All these data come under the heading of **monitoring**. What is needed is an additional suite of programs which runs together with the CALL package and collects the relevant data.

The information which can be reported is of two principal types: assessment data and error data. The assessment data are essentially the students' scores, plus any relevant information about the attaining of the scores – for instance, how many times a particular student attempted the package, how long the session/s lasted, and so on. The error data cover the errors the student makes, together with background information such as the questions answered incorrectly even at a second attempt, questions where the time limit was exceeded, and so on. This information represents some of the most important information which the teacher registers in everyday classroom teaching. A simple set of assessment data for a conventional exercise might appear as follows:

Student name	Date	Time spent	Result (%)
Bell, Mary	4-Mar-84	00:51:32	51
	5-Mar-84	00:32:07	91
Green, Fred	1-Mar-84	01:01:21	36

Here Mary Bell has improved her score by taking the lesson a second time, while Fred Green has only had one attempt and has done rather badly. Data can, of course, be presented in a different lay-out according to the teacher's requirements.

Numerical information need not be exclusively orientated towards the individual student. It is possible to collect information for one particular CALL package, so as to record the total range of marks, information on first attempts of questions, on averages over all attempts and so on. A CALL programme which results in generally low scores is obviously more difficult, or less successfully presented, than others. Unpredictable and violent variations in results may indicate incomplete comprehension of basic concepts on the part of the students.

In addition to numerical information about the student's progress, monitoring can also present the teacher with information about the errors students make along the way. There are two main kinds of error data: anticipated (or 'trapped') wrong answers and other wrong answers. Trapped wrong answers are incorrect answers which the teacher has specifically anticipated and singled out for comment, remedial material, and possible retaking by the student. It is helpful to have a record of trapped errors which were indeed made by students to check whether the teacher has anticipated correctly.

A record of the untrapped wrong answers is also very useful. It is here that the teacher will identify oversights or unclear points in the formulation of questions, as well as cases where the student simply does not understand. If the untrapped wrong answers are very systematic, or show a preference for certain types of errors, the teacher should probably include these errors in the trapped answer specification in order to give the student the most positive and useful help as early as possible. The error data may also be useful for research purposes in language learning.

There are, then, two fundamental ways in which the reporting of data can be organized. One is orientated towards the student (assessment), and the other towards the lesson (evaluation). Collection of error data may help the teacher to spot an individual student's problems, as well as to identify the most frequently occurring error types. But there is a real problem of ethics as well as a pragmatic problem here. Students are sufficiently concerned about an impersonal system collecting their marks. They are sometimes even more concerned about the system making a permanent record of their errors. This situation must be handled by the teacher with discretion and tact, since the collecting of errors is in the student's interest. This presupposes, of course, that the teacher has the time and inclination to analyse the errors. However, there is no compulsion about monitoring, in spite of its general usefulness. Some teachers never use monitoring, leaving the student to use CALL programs as and when required and to draw the appropriate conclusions from the scores given (see section 5.2.4). Students using such a system have reported that one of the major advantages of CALL was that they could work freely without being too concerned by possible errors (whereas in the classroom they would hold back: Demaizière 1983:11–12). The decision whether or not to monitor depends on the role CALL is playing in the course, and on the other types of assessment employed. Of course, it need not be an all-or-nothing decision. Some packages can be for private study while others can be monitored. Other exercises of a more exploratory type, such as simulations, are simply unsuitable for assessment monitoring.

Finally, the teacher should be aware that smaller microcomputers may simply not have enough physical memory to handle all the information which the teacher wants (though Michael Carr and Roy Bivon at the University of East Anglia have achieved impressive results using a microcomputer with two disc drives). Advances in hardware suggest that within five years or so the basic microcomputer will be a much more powerful machine. At the present time, however, restrictions on physical memory constitute a genuine and serious limitation on the ability of some CALL systems to report back data to the teacher.

Having said that, one should add that much of the assessment data is as useful to the student – for self-assessment purposes – as it is to the teacher. Researchers as well as teachers have found CALL monitoring facilities useful. For instance, Curtin, Avner & Provenzano (1981) have tried to establish a model of the learner, and ultimately to describe the optimal conditions for learning to take place, by monitoring students using a number of CALL programs on the PLATO system for the teaching of Russian at the University of Illinois (see section 7.5).

7.4   The integration of CALL into language teaching

Language teaching tends in practice to be eclectic: there are not only exceptionally many paths and educational means for arriving at a given educational goal, but there are also very many types of educational materials which can be used to achieve that goal. To complicate matters even further, there are many different goals, and views about the goals which language teaching is supposed to aim at. It therefore serves little purpose to talk of integrating CALL into the language-teaching prog- ramme in any standardized way. However, it is useful to consider some of the possibilities offered by CALL.

In section 7.2 we outlined some of the areas in language teaching where CALL could profitably be employed. In this sense, there has already been some discussion of how to integrate CALL into the language syllabus. Yet certain other decisions remain. In this section we concentrate on some of the organizational possibilities for the integration of CALL. Such possibi- lities include CALL for private study, CALL in the main classroom, the use of a special CALL laboratory, and CALL for individual or group work.

One of the most obvious and accessible benefits of CALL is its capacity to provide personalized and self-paced learning. This allows students of varying ability enough flexibility to find their own level, which is a boon to slow learners and fast learners who need remedial and extension exercises respectively. Students who are reluctant classroom learners may also benefit. Such personalized learning has become fashionable in educa- tional writings over the last decade, signalling a movement towards a more flexible organization of learning, in which much greater emphasis is placed on the differing learning styles and abilities of individuals.

Rapid learners, who cover the ground faster than their peers and consistently achieve better results, may become disenchanted or bored with the CALL medium, particularly if it fails to extend their capacities. Letting such students advance at full speed into the following week's material is not a good policy, since it creates all kinds of problems of co-ordination. A better plan is to provide some extension materials for such students in order to retain their interest and curiosity, and to develop their language skills. An able student may even be asked to write CALL programs. Such an exercise harnesses the enthusiasm of certain students for computers in general, and also provides ample opportunity for insights into the complexities of natural language.

An extension of the private-study facility which CALL can provide is the use of CALL packages in the learner's home. The popularity of home computers, especially in Britain, means that an increasing number of students will have direct access to a computer. The student may even borrow a 'home' computer from the resources centre at school or from a neighbour. While such a development has obvious advantages, it also reduces the degree of control which can be exercised by the teacher. Monitoring is, for instance, less feasible. Far more serious is the danger that learners will be exposed to bad CALL material from the local computer shop, although there is no reason why good software should not also be on sale. A possible solution is for teachers to organize a lending system, along the lines of a library, for well-tested CALL packages. This presupposes that the material used in the school, college, and so on, is compatible with the learner's machine at home. Unfortunately, this is frequently not the case. Such a lack of co-ordination is currently a hallmark of CALL. The problem will not be rectified, or at least simplified, until local education authorities, publishing houses and software producers decide to co-ordinate their activities.

Within the educational institution itself there are two principal ways of physically organizing the CALL component of the course. Either the CALL facilities can all be located in one room (a CALL laboratory), or they can be distributed throughout ordinary classrooms. If a particular institution has only one microcomputer, then the problem scarcely arises – unless it is a question of prising the machine from the grip of teachers in the numerate disciplines. Microcomputers can of course be moved from one room to another, so any particular location of the microcomputer need not be permanent. An additional choice is whether to allow each machine to be used independently, or whether to give the teacher central control through a networked system (see section 2.1.5). (Note that with a network the facilities can equally well be in one room or distributed over a wider area.) A recent report from the United States on the use of microcomputers in schools (Blomeyer 1984) favours networking, since less of the teacher's time is taken up with 'management' tasks such as distributing and recovering students' discs. It is also noted that networking may prevent students from tampering with programs. However, it is not easy to network some microcomputer systems, so this option is not always a viable one. Furthermore, some teachers may decide that the benefits of allowing students greater freedom outweigh the possible costs.

The advantages of a CALL laboratory (or CAL laboratory, if it is to be

117

shared with other departments) are perhaps largely of a practical nature. Security precautions are, for instance, much simpler if all the computers or terminals are located in one place. It also makes more sense to have a CALL laboratory if the teacher wishes to spend an identifiable part of each week's lessons working on CALL with the whole class. This is a pedagogical decision, but one which has practical consequences. Private study may also be easier to organize if all machines are located centrally. However, such an arrangement could be counter-productive in other respects.

Locating all the CALL facilities in a room of their own could well have the effect of destroying the very flexibility offered by CALL. Having a special location for CALL activities has the psychological disadvantage of marking it out as an activity separate from the rest of the course. One weekly timetable slot located in the CALL room might also make both teacher and students feel obliged to make use of the equipment come what may – regardless of present need and inclination. If CALL is to be used in normal class time, it seems more likely that it will be put to its best use if it is fully integrated physically into the language-teaching classroom; it can then also be pedagogically integrated. This means that various language-learning activities can be accommodated in the classroom simultaneously, of which CALL will be one. This is in keeping with recent developments in language teaching, where there is a move away from the heavy concentration on formal classroom teaching with its constant central focus on the teacher. The presentation of a range of activities in the classroom also solves the problem of what to do if you have only one machine available: it can be used by students in rotation, either individually or in groups. Another solution if only one computer is available for a whole class, is to connect it to a large video-screen. The teacher can discuss with the class each step as they work through the program together. Unfortunately, video-screens can be more expensive than the microcomputer.

Even if the teacher has made the decision to have some CALL facilities in the classroom, there are still a number of alternative ways in which these can be used. These include work by individual students, pairs or groups. Obviously some programs are better suited to individual use, for example, a vocabulary game such as Snap, where a speedy reaction is required. In other cases it may be a question of convenience for classroom management, or a question of personal preference on the part of the students. Some prefer collaborative work, others are lone wolves. Some packages where complex decisions are required may be more suited to small-group work. Such decisions may be explicitly linguistic, in which case students may need to test rules on each other in their negotiation of a response (e.g. Johns's S-ENDING). Alternatively, if the linguistic aim of the package is more covert, for example, an adventure game where the foreign language is the main medium of presentation and operation, then certain negotiations may be carried out between students in the foreign language before a decision on the next step is reached. In such an exercise, the computer is acting as a prompt to further language use.

Given a good monitoring system with facilities for scoring and timing, the teacher can even organize competitions between students with just one machine. Students can volunteer themselves for their turn when they are ready. This may even beat official 'tests' for encouraging students to do revision (depending on their level of self-motivation or sophistication).

7.5 How effective is CALL?

One of the main problems in evaluating CALL (and CAL in general) is the number of variables involved. Indeed, this applies to all evaluations of particular teaching techniques. Such questions as teacher motivation, method of testing, size of group, size of institution, age and social background of learners, amount of private study, and so on, can be of vital importance. However, it is virtually impossible to control all such variables. An additional factor to be borne in mind when considering evaluation reports is whether sufficient information is given about the methods used to measure student attainment, and about the relationship between such tests and the stated teaching objectives.

In a review of evaluation studies of CAL in general, Kulik, Kulik & Cohen (1980) claim that 'computer-based' or 'computer-supplemented' instruction has educational advantages at elementary and secondary school levels. The main advantage claimed seems to be 'performance gains of 1-8 months over children who received only traditional instruction' (1980:526). The position for college level education is, however, not so clear. The majority of research on CAL in general has been in the use of CAL in tutorial mode as a complete substitute for normal tuition. Overall Kulik *et al.* claim that the fifty-nine evaluation studies they considered show the following results for computer-based instruction:

(a) it raised examination scores by about three percentage points;
(b) it had small positive effects on attitudes of college students towards instruction and subject matter;
(c) when substituted for conventional teaching it reduced tuition time by about two thirds.

However, as Kulik *et al.* point out, the benefits claimed are not as impressive as those claimed for other innovations such as the Keller system (see Kulik, Kulik & Cohen 1979), but are comparable to those claimed for programmed instruction.

Ever since the earliest explorations in CALL, the computer's presence and role have been subject to constant scrutiny and challenge. Many language teachers have felt that the very nature of the computer is contrary to the essence of language learning. And among those who admit the relevance of the computer, many have questioned its effectiveness.

The educational effectiveness of CALL is still a controversial issue. We can now see more clearly what kinds of language-learning tasks can be handled by the computer. But the nature and extent of the computer's *qualitative* contribution to the language-learning experience is not clear. The information that we do have rests mainly on surveys of students' attitudes to their experiences with CALL. Typical surveys reveal positive student reactions for motivation and continued enrolment, the quantity of learning, the pace of learning, and the type of language skills learnt (McEwen 1977; Taylor 1979). Some of these positive results are probably encouraged by the novelty factor of working with a new educational technology. The reverse phenomenon is known as the 'pall factor', when the novelty begins to wear off, and some of the computer's more vulnerable failings – particularly in an unimaginative and repetitive use of drill facilities – can do much harm to the quality and quantity of the students' learning. In general, however, students react positively to CALL, and to its most characteristic advantages of personalized, self-access, self-pacing and distance learning. They also value highly the computer's ability to interact, and to deliver high-quality feedback instantly.

If the qualitative benefits of CALL are still to be fully demonstrated, its *quantitative* advantages have been better researched in a number of CALL projects, most of them in the United States. Some of the results have been equivocal or inconclusive: either the number of students has been too small, or the results themselves have not shown any appreciable difference with students using CALL. Curtin, Dawson, Provenzano & Cooper (1976), for instance, used the PLATO system to teach a reading–translation course in Russian, and found that there was no significant difference in the performance of PLATO and non-PLATO students. Although the CALL students were more likely to include the highest grades, they were also more susceptible to deferral and dropout. Curtin *et al.* ascribe this feature to insufficient classroom contact, a factor which has been confirmed elsewhere for students taking intensive CALL courses (Hartnett 1974).

Most of the other published evaluations of CALL, however, have been more positive. Fairly typical are the results obtained by Rosenbaum (1968) with students of German: one group took a conventional audio-lingual course supplemented with language-laboratory exercises, while for another group CAI work replaced the language laboratory; the classwork was aimed mainly at audio-lingual learning. He concludes that the CAI group performed roughly as well on the listening/speaking skills (MLA Foreign Language Cooperative Subtests) as the non-CAI group, which had done language-laboratory exercises. However, as he rightly points out, this could be attributed to the ineffectiveness of the language laboratory rather than any superiority of CAI. As might be expected, the CAI group significantly outperformed the non-CAI group in reading/writing skills, since this is what they had been practising in CAI.

Rosenbaum draws attention to the volume and quality of individual interaction between the student and computer in CAI, as compared to student–teacher interaction in the classroom. He estimates that a student in a fiteen-member class may have five personal interactions with the teacher during a fifty-minute class; when working with a computer the figure is at least ten times greater. Measured in terms of time of active attention, a student in a nine-strong class might achieve between 3.6 and 1.7 minutes in a fifty-minute class; in a fifty-minute CAI session the figure is again at least ten times better. To this is added the volume of personalized information and feedback which the student receives.

Motivation is unquestionably an important factor in language learning (see section 4.3.2). CALL may well have a role to play here. One useful index of the popularity of CALL is the continuing enrolment rate of students. Suppes & Morningstar (1969) report a 72 per cent continuing enrolment rate for CAI students versus 32 per cent for non-CAI students in elementary Russian classes at Stanford University. Even where the figures have been less remarkable, in almost all cases there is a significantly greater number of students from CALL groups who re-enrol than from non-CALL control groups. The exception is the intensive CALL courses mentioned above.

There is evidence of the efficacy of CALL over a whole range of learning activities. Atkinson (1968), Morrison & Adams (1968), and Rosenbaum (1968) all report significantly improved performance from CAI students in almost all areas of learning tasks. And even when the improvement was not statistically significant, there are apparently no instances where the CAI group performed significantly worse than non-CAI groups. Many kinds of tests were used: vocabulary recognition and production, reading, pronunciation, recognition of regular and nonsense words, and several others. The CAI students not only performed better; they had (perhaps predictably) covered more of the learning material, in a shorter time, and with greater retention and improved learning strategies.

One general point worth noting is that students' attitudes towards CALL work appear to improve if they have previous experience of computer literacy courses. Blomeyer (1984:7–8) reports that students with no such experience needed more instruction in class on operating the computer, and 'sometimes demonstrated unrealistic expectations of the microcomputer's contribution to learning, sometimes an outright aversion to their use'. This indicates that a clear policy towards the educational use of computers needs to be developed across an institution as a whole if full benefit is to be gained from CALL, and indeed from CAL in general.

In conclusion, CAI/CALL packages have largely been judged effective within the range of activities mentioned, and within the specified objectives of particular types of exercise, although evaluation of exploratory problem-solving and simulation exercises has scarcely begun.

7.6 Conclusion

In this chapter we have shown some of the ways in which CALL can enrich the classroom environment. We have indicated that the computer cannot replace the human teacher, nor is it desirable that it should. The use of language is ultimately, after all, an activity which involves human beings with other human beings. However, such considerations do not invalidate the use of CALL in the classroom, nor do the technological limitations of the computer (for instance, its current limitations in processing speech input). In spite of the restrictions, the computer has an important place in language learning and teaching. We have tried to show what that place is at the present time. In the next chapter we consider ways in which some of its technical limitations are being overcome and its potential role is being enlarged.

8 Developing areas

In this book we have been mainly concerned with what the computer can offer the language teacher at present, using standard equipment in the most obvious ways. There are, however, more adventurous possibilities which go well beyond those considered so far. The first two developments described below involve using the computer as a data bank to store lexical material (section 8.1) or to store running text (section 8.2). From the computing side, everything necessary for these uses is already available, though experience here is limited. Our third section is more speculative; it concerns developments in linguistics and in artificial intelligence (section 8.3). While the first three sections involve more ambitious uses of technology which is already available, the remaining sections deal with various devices which are more specialized or less readily available than the standard equipment. They will extend the range of CALL into sound (section 8.4) and graphic images and pictures (section 8.5).

8.1 The computer as a dictionary

As mentioned earlier, the computer is able to store and manipulate large amounts of data. This is particularly true of mainframes, but minis and micros have increasingly impressive storage capabilities. One obvious set of data for language teaching is a dictionary (monolingual, bilingual or multilingual). Computerized dictionaries have been used by textbook writers for some time and they played a central role in Alford's work (see section 3.1.4). However, dictionaries can now be made available for the student to use interactively; the student types in a word and the computer responds with its meanings. This is a valuable resource because, in the course of learning a language, students spend a great deal of time simply turning the pages of dictionaries (timing the number of minutes spent during an hour can give a very high figure, see Ahmad, Corbett & Edwards 1978:39). The computer, because of its rapid response, saves a considerable amount of time, and students enjoy using it in this way. The entries can be presented as in a standard dictionary, with alternative meanings, examples and grammatical information. The difference lies in the computer's rapid search facilities; moreover, additions and alterations to the dictionary can be easily made.

These features can be illustrated by a computerized dictionary designed and implemented by Jean Edwards at the University of Surrey. The software was written in response to a request from students who had been actively involved in the development of CALL material. They complained that every student in their group spent a good deal of time looking up words to do a weekly translation. They wanted just one to do the spadework (on a rota basis). A program was written to allow a student, sitting at a terminal with a conventional dictionary, to create a computer file containing the required words together with their meanings. This file could then be looked up by the other students by giving the title of the translation passage. When a new word was encountered, the student typed it in and the computer gave its meaning. As the computer is scanning a small list, the response time is extremely fast.

If this were the full extent of the system, then we would have only a computerized version of the list of words which follows a text in a traditional textbook. However, the computer has a larger dictionary as a back-up. (This can be built up gradually from the individual lists, as we shall see below.) If a student asks for a word which is not included in the word list, then the computer automatically refers to the larger dictionary. This system combines the advantages of the small dictionary (rapid response) with the greater coverage of a larger dictionary.

The small dictionaries for individual texts and the larger back-up dictionary interact in two further ways. When a small dictionary is being created, the computer first checks whether required words are in the large dictionary and, if so, it offers meanings. Further meanings can be added if required. When the small dictionary has been created (probably from a combination of words already in the back-up dictionary and of words entered directly into the new small dictionary) it can be checked and corrected where necessary. The teacher can then merge the contents of the small dictionary into the back-up. The small dictionary can still be used as long as required, but the new words are made part of the back-up dictionary and so are available for reference when different texts are being read. In this way the back-up dictionary can be gradually expanded. The programming involved, with details of the storage and the search techniques employed, is described in Edwards (1981). Since the computer system used had rather limited storage capacity, the software was designed so that the dictionary entries utilized the minimum amount of computer memory (by 'data packing'). The search programs, for locating words and their associated meanings in the word list and master dictionary, used sophisticated search and pattern-matching techniques to maintain a fast response time.

As mentioned earlier, once the data are stored in the computer, they are available for use in various different ways. One suggestion made by Edwards is that after a session using the dictionary, the student should be offered a vocabulary test by the computer, based on the items looked up. Another suggestion (P. T. Culhane, personal communication) is to have every entry in the computer dictionary marked according to its frequency of occurrence; for example, the most common 1000 words might be labelled as class I, the second 1000 as type II, and the rest as class III. On logging in, the student would be asked to indicate the level reached in the language. This information could then be used when displaying glosses: for example, if an advanced student asked for one of the most common 1000 words, this would be highlighted as a word to be learned immediately. Once the computer contains a dictionary with entries labelled according to bands of frequency in this way, it can provide random vocabulary tests at a level appropriate to a particular student (for example, excluding words occurring in the first 1000 for an advanced student). Information on word frequencies, readily available in this way, would also be useful for the teacher in choosing and adapting teaching texts.

It is easy to think of uses for such a dictionary. The difficulty is rather the mundane problem of how to input it into the computer. The way described above is to build up the main dictionary gradually from the word lists for individual texts: thus the back-up dictionary for a particular text consists of all the words previously entered for other texts. Alternatively, given the publisher's consent, one can take an existing dictionary and patiently type it in. Or, more accurately and less tediously, one can use an **optical character reader** (a costly device which actually reads a written text into the computer). Once in the computer, the dictionary can always be updated and improved – new meanings can be added, lexical and grammatical difficulties can be pointed out. In the future we can hope to have computer dictionaries available off the shelf. Printed dictionaries are increasingly being set up on computers and then printed from computer files. We must hope that publishers will make dictionaries available in machine-readable form (on magnetic tape or floppy disc), which will allow teachers to use the best dictionaries without the problem of how to get the dictionary into the computer. To date, co-operative publishers have given copies of such dictionaries on an informal basis.

A number of microcomputer systems offer word-processing facilities which help the user to lay out a document and edit text. Some of these systems also include a list of English words (70,000 or even more) together with programs to match the text typed against the entries in the word list and to highlight words which do not match, for the user to check whether an error has been made. These **spelling checkers** are not very expensive and they have a potential role in various free-composition exercises. Of course, the next logical step is to implement full dictionaries, including bilingual dictionaries, as part of word-processing packages; the systems available to date are rather expensive.

Major organizations which require large amounts of translation, particularly of a technical or specialized nature, are becoming aware of the computer's potential and are increasingly setting up **term banks** (lists of specialist terms with their recognized translations and perhaps also an explanation) on computers. This is often part of an attempt to standardize terminology and so to improve the clarity of translations. It is virtually certain that professional translators will soon be working with computerized dictionary facilities as a matter of course. For the advanced language student an introduction to this technology would be a valuable asset for a career involving languages.

8.2 Running text stored on the computer

The other type of data which can fruitfully be stored on the computer is continuous text – a corpus. The texts which make up the corpus may be an unstructured collection, or they may be grouped according to thematic variety or the type of language used. Such texts are already available in machine-readable form, especially for English, but also for other languages, for the cost of the magnetic tape onto which they are copied (see the 'Useful addresses' section). The availability of a corpus makes possible some linguistic projects which create an invaluable interplay between learning the language and learning about the language.

Let us take a straightforward example: imagine a foreign learner of English who is surprised and interested by the plural verb in a sentence like: *The committee have decided.* A teacher who wanted to take advantage of this interest might suggest that the student should find out something about this construction and write up the results. The student can look in textbooks where, in many cases, examples will be found to support whatever rule the grammarian favours; native speakers are another source of information but they may well give the form which they think ought to be used rather than the form they actually use. If a corpus is available on a computer, then it is possible to scan it for suitable examples. The machine will not understand a command to: 'look for examples of verb agreement with nouns like *committee*'. The command will be equivalent to the following: 'find occurrences of *committee, government, team* ... and print them together with twenty words on each side of the occurrence'. Other nouns which take this type of agreement could be added to the list. In the sample provided by the computer there will be a considerable number of examples which are of no use: the noun may not be in subject position, or the verb may be in the simple past tense. In fact, this particular problem was tackled and a test run yielded a substantial number of relevant examples from which the student could investigate the factors which make the plural agreement more or less likely. The computer, then, has done the spadework to allow the student to concentrate on a particular problem of English – to examine a set of sentences of the same type, and to learn something about English syntax and style. The actual scanning can be done on some computers simply by using the software provided for locating and changing items in stored files (the editor). A more flexible alternative is to use a set of programs such as the Oxford Concordance Program (Hockey & Marriott 1980). This package can produce concordances, indexes or word lists with frequencies; it can scan for word combinations, detach prefixes and suffixes and so sort by root (allowing interesting morphological projects); and it is specifically designed to take into account the various problems posed by diacritic symbols and non-Roman scripts. In this way the tools of computational linguistics (see section 3.3) can be used for CALL purposes.

Project work of the type just described is likely to involve the student in using the computer as more than just a CALL machine. The Oxford Concordance Program is intended for those with little knowledge of computing, but, unlike CALL packages, it still involves the student in a certain amount of computing. This should not worry us, since an increasing proportion of jobs requires familiarity with computers. Yet it is still possible for students to leave school and higher education with little notion of what computers are. If the language teacher, while deepening students' knowledge of the language, also introduces them to computing (and to linguistics), then this can only be of benefit to the students (cf. Wilkes 1979:11).

8.3 Advances in linguistics and in artificial intelligence

The previous section helped to illustrate the way in which language teaching and linguistics are linked. It is clear that any development in linguistics which genuinely deepens our understanding of language will be of potential interest to those involved in CALL. More explicit and more accurate descriptions of the languages we teach will provide the raw material for better CALL packages. Theoretical advances may give us a clearer picture of the nature of language and so of the task which faces the language learner. When we turn to the branch of applied linguistics which considers language learning, then the links with CALL are even more evident. Information on how learners learn most effectively will be invaluable. It is not simply a matter of CALL benefiting from applied linguistics, however. The computer can, if desired, keep very detailed records of how CALL programs are used. Conventional monitoring has already been discussed (section 7.3). For research purposes, data can be stored on the path taken by the learner through a branching program, the time taken over every response, the exact form of every error made (not just the number), the patterns of the errors, and so on. In this way CALL can provide more detailed data than have generally been available to the applied linguist in the past.

While the potential value of linguistics for CALL hardly needs to be spelt out, the relevance of artificial intelligence may require more explanation. Many CALL programs appear impressive when one sees them running at a terminal. In most cases, however, they are very restricted in scope: the topic is limited and the author has to anticipate every possible student response to every prompt. Consider again GERAD. It appears to 'know' something about German adjectives; it can give the correct adjectival form in sixty sentences and can display the paradigms. But it does not 'work out' the form required for a particular sentence from the information in the tables; it merely stores it. Given a new German sentence, GERAD could not predict the correct form of the adjectival endings; in other words, it cannot do what it asks the student to do. Some CALL programs are more 'intelligent' (in the sense that they 'exhibit behavior that we call intelligent behavior when we observe it in human beings' Slagle 1971:1). There are morphological programs which store stems and endings separately and add the appropriate ending to a given stem as required. Such programs 'know' a little about the language. Other programs determine the path taken through the material according to the student's responses; for example, incorrect answers make the program branch to explanatory or remedial material. Programs like this 'know' a little about teaching.

Those working in artificial intelligence set their sights much higher than this. They aim to develop intelligent systems (Intelligent Computer Aided Instruction or ICAI systems) which would include a representation of the subject matter, the ability to carry on a dialogue with the student and the capability to use student errors to diagnose misunderstandings. Barr & Feigenbaum (1982:229–35) discuss such systems in terms of three modules. The first is the **expertise module**. This component includes a representation of the subject matter; it also generates problems and evaluates student responses. The **student-model module** represents the student's understanding of the material: it may gain information from direct questions, from analysing student responses and from assumptions about the student's experience and the difficulty of the subject matter. The third component, the **tutoring module**, is the one that communicates with the student: it selects problems, monitors performance and provides assistance and remedial material.

There is no prospect of such ambitious packages being implemented in the immediate future; furthermore, much of the research is in areas that are more obviously geared to problem solving than is CALL. Nevertheless, the ICAI model is valuable as a goal and as a source for suggesting the next steps forward. Let us therefore review the three modules from the perspective of CALL.

The expertise module for CALL purposes would contain a knowledge base of part of the target language – a lexicon, rules of semantics and syntax and so on. It would use this base to generate exercises and to analyse the student's responses. While a full representation is a long way off, various computational linguists have successfully represented fragments of natural languages (for example, the verbal morphology of a particular language) on computers; the best-known work is that of Winograd (1972; 1983). The most pressing need for CALL in this area is for more sophisticated processing of the student's input (see Hart 1981b:17, and references there). At present it is normally the *form* of the response which determines the direction which the program will take. This accounts for the greater difficulty in devising CALL materials for more advanced students; given a reasonable command of the language, the student can give several plausible responses to a prompt and these responses may be radically different in terms of their linguistic structure. We must look forward to processing of the response in semantic terms, which opens exciting perspectives for CALL. It will allow the learner to take a much more active role (cf. Goodyear & Barnard 1982:69–71). The student-model module would represent the student's grasp of the foreign language, constantly updating itself from the student's work with the computer. It would ensure that the CALL sessions were directed in the most helpful way for the student and, since this module would be available for reference by the teacher, more fruitful classwork would be possible. The tutoring module would interact directly with the student – in natural language. A great deal of research is being invested in the problem of natural-language communication with computers (see section 3.3): CALL will be in a privileged position as the expertise module will be of direct relevance here. The tutoring module should guide the student in the most helpful way, giving advice, clues and remedial help where necessary. For an example of work in this area see Cerri & Breuker (1981); for a general discussion of ICAI see O'Shea & Self (1983:127–76).

The day when a computer consistently gives helpful advice to a language learner in natural language is a long way off. Nevertheless, research towards this goal will have spin-offs of value for CALL. And we must retain the aim of creating CALL programs which 'know' more about natural language, which are responsive to the work of individual students and which give the maximum amount of help to the learner.

8.4 Speech input/output

There are two main areas of technical innovation which are of special relevance to the language teacher: speech input/output and graphics.

Only a few years ago these were the domain of research scientists and engineers. It has been estimated, however, that the cost of the hardware associated with such ventures has been decreasing by as much as 50 per cent per year. Technological developments are generally greeted with optimism. However, it soon becomes clear that a language teacher confronted with new technology has to ask two questions: how does it fit into the curriculum? and how practical is the device? We will try to answer these questions as we consider those aspects of speech input/output and graphics which are relevant for CALL purposes. (For a discussion of the likely impact of future developments in hardware and software on CAL in general, see Fields & Paris 1981.)

Most CALL programs are concerned with the written word. On the one hand, this serves as a useful counterbalance to the recent trend in which innovation in language teaching has been concentrated on oral/ aural skills. On the other hand, language involves first and foremost the activities of speaking and listening, so naturally those involved in CALL have tried to incorporate the spoken element. Even relatively small micro-computers often have sockets for output leads which can be connected to other equipment, which the computer can then control. Keen teenagers and their teachers have produced micro-controlled train sets, robots and so on. Language teachers have been more interested in computer-controlled tape-recorders and have, at various times, connected tape-recorders to computers to give an aural component to CALL (for example, Adams, Morrison & Reddy 1968).

These developments, though certainly interesting, remained largely local. Two main reasons may be suggested. The first was that the tape-recorder, with its various moving parts and its tapes which had to be threaded by hand (and stopped when rewinding), was not an ideal partner for the computer. The advent of the cassette-recorder reduced this problem considerably. More serious, however, was the fact that in most cases the computers and tape-recorders were connected up differently in various institutions. Now Tandberg have produced a cassette-recorder which incorporates a microprocessor and is specifically designed to be driven by an external computer. The microprocessor controls the tape, and it does so extremely accurately. Thus, if the computer is running a CALL program, the cassette-recorder can be instructed to find a particular point in a recorded text (say the gap between two words) and the microprocessor will find that point without fail, irrespective of the point to which the tape has been wound. The program could first play a passage on the tape and then display a question on the screen. The student would type an answer. If correct, there would be another question, or another passage on the tape. If the answer was incorrect, the relevant section of the passage could be played again and the question repeated. Or a different section of the tape could be played (not previously heard) where the same content was given in a different or simpler form. By linking cassette-recorders of this type to a central microcomputer, with a headset, keyboard and monitor for each student, one would arrive at a computerized language laboratory. Each position combines the usual language laboratory equipment with a CALL work-station. The laboratory could be used as a conventional language laboratory, or CALL programs of the type just described could be loaded from the teacher's microcomputer in the console on to the individual positions to permit CALL work. The point is that, unlike the conventional language laboratory, the computerized version responds differently to different student responses (via the keyboard). It allows a branching program because it combines a relatively fast-winding cassette-recorder with a microprocessor as a standard piece of equipment. The future will tell how successful this innovation will be. Its fate depends on the reliability and price of the equipment and on the quality of the CALL materials produced for it.

Cassette-recorders are a slow-speed device for storing and retrieving data; they are limited by the speed at which the tape can be wound. Search times can be greatly improved if one uses instead a random-access audio device (Hart 1981b:4), which has a floppy disc instead of a tape. The great advantage is the speed with which speech can be retrieved from any part of the disc. In other words, the search does not have to start from the beginning – the right spot can be found directly. This device is not widely used. When recordable audiodiscs become commercially available for domestic use, this may have a beneficial spin-off for CALL. However, instead of recording on to a special disc, as this device does, it is also possible to record on to an ordinary computer disc. Compared with cassette-recorders, disc drives are very significantly faster, and the smaller number of moving parts makes them more reliable. It is already possible to supplement a microcomputer with a collection of hardware and software modules which enable the computer to record and play back sound. The CALL system thereby becomes an audiovisual system. It should be stressed that this system, like the language laboratory, can only talk *to* the student. While the student can respond orally, the computer cannot understand and respond. (Research is going on into speech-recognition systems. The problem is complex because human speech is acoustically so varied and rich; the system will literally have to be trained to 'understand' individual speakers, thus making the whole enterprise expensive in terms of both human and computer resources. Once the human utterance has been successfully 'heard', there is still the major problem of understanding it. We will therefore concentrate on speech-output systems.)

The hardware module of a speech-input/output system typically consists of special-purpose circuit boards, disc drive(s), a microphone, loudspeakers and various connections to interface the computer system with the hardware modules. The software modules consist of programs which enable a language teacher to digitize and then store human speech and facilitate the playback of the digitized speech through a loudspeaker. The digitization of human speech involves the conversion of electrical impulses generated by the microphone into numbers. This is accomplished by the special-purpose circuit boards mentioned above. The circuit boards convert the sound signals ('analog') to numbers at the recording stage and convert the digital signal back to analog at the playback stage. Once the additional circuit boards are in place, the microphone and loudspeaker are then plugged into the proper socket. The computer appears to function as a cassette-recorder – it records speech and replays it when required. The difference is that instead of recording speech on a tape, it records it as a long string of numbers: there is no moving tape. However, this is not 'robot' speech. The quality available on a micro-computer is similar to that found on a cassette-recorder.

A microcomputer with speech output equipment

Once the speech is digitized (stored as a set of numbers), the spoken phrases or words can be used as items of data in the same way as text data: that is to say they can be used at will as part of a CALL program. The first obvious application is to add speech output to ordinary CALL programs. A question–answer program could not only display correct answers on the screen, but could 'say' the answer at the same time. Many CALL programs can be readily adapted in this way. The audio element is a useful addition, which ensures that the student hears the correct pronunciation of a form as it appears on the screen.

Speech output also makes possible quite different CALL exercises. An interesting type is that of sound discrimination. A foreign language often presents phonetic difficulties specific to speakers of a given native language; thus English /r/ and /w/ are difficult for speakers of languages which do not distinguish them. Before pronouncing the sounds correctly, the student must be able to distinguish them confidently. The teacher could set up a CALL program as follows. First the digital input system is used to record a set of words which include /r/ or /w/. Then a simple program is written to work in the following way. It looks up the recorded set of words, selects one word and plays it through the audio system. The screen displays the question: 'Does this word include an /r/ or a /w/? Answer R or W, or if you would like to hear the word again type A.' The computer 'says' the word again if required (several times if necessary), informs the student whether the sound was correctly identified and then moves on to the next word. The words can be arranged so that the first few include the /r/ or /w/ in initial position, followed by examples in more difficult phonetic environments. (Alternatively they can be presented in random order, rather than in the same fixed order, so that the exercise can be used on several occasions.)

There are several advantages in using a computer in this way. First, the inability to identify sounds troubles many students – they feel inadequate or fear that it results from a hearing difficulty. In such circumstances it may be easier to work with a machine than with a human. Compared with a cassette-recorder the computer has two advantages: first, it can tell the student immediately whether or not a sound was correctly identified; second, there are no moving parts, no knobs to operate, no tapes to thread. In particular, the computer can repeat a word or phrase as often as is required without perceptible delay – there is no tape to wind back. This is because individual words are stored as digital data and each can be called and output just as a set of written words can be called and output via the screen.

It is also possible to associate the recorded words with their written equivalents. This makes possible a sort of dictation exercise: the computer 'says' a word (repeating it if required), the student types it in and the computer assesses the answer. This procedure could be valuable for those learning the troublesome orthography of English. Perhaps the program should include sympathetic and humorous responses for sensible though incorrect answers.

It might appear that speech output offers considerable advantages. However, the examples given above used individual words as output rather than, for example, long texts for comprehension. There is a practical limitation at present in that the amount of speech which can be stored is restricted: on a microcomputer one might hope to store a few minutes of speech in total, but not all in one stretch.

The reason for this is as follows. We stated earlier that computer-generated speech requires that the speech be recorded not as analog signals (as on a gramophone record), but as digital signals (numbers in binary code), which correspond to the waveforms of the sounds of speech. A high-quality representation of speech requires very large quantities of such numbers: a second of speech may well require 10,000 or 20,000 numbers, each number occupying one or even two computer words (see section 2.1.1).

The digital patterns of the sound-waves, the binary numbers mentioned above, are processed by the central processing unit of the computer system. The CPU has a fast but relatively small memory, comprising around 65,000 computer words on a typical microcomputer system, though not all of them are available to the user. The main memory is fast, because any of its 65,000 computer words, for example, can be retrieved in a few microseconds. Once processed, the numbers are stored on a peripheral storage device, which has a larger but slower memory. An ordinary floppy disc, for instance, can store about 500,000 computer words, but each word takes three to ten times longer to retrieve than it takes to retrieve it from CPU memory. All this means that, at the recording stage, speech items are recorded in quantities of three or four seconds a time. The processed item is 'dumped' on the disc, which may take as much as nine to twelve seconds. One can store up to a few minutes of speech in total on the floppy disc. The problem arises at the playback stage. The CALL program instructs the CPU to obtain a sound from the disc drive; for each second of speech it may take as much as three to ten seconds to load the digital pattern of the sound from the peripheral device into the main (CPU) memory.

For present purposes, we are limited to storing a relatively small number of words, and outputting them as single words or phrases. This means in effect that speech output can either be an addition to a conventional CALL program, or it can be used in the ways described earlier, where the teaching method required only single words. (The random-access audio disc mentioned above allows about twenty-three minutes of continuous speech.) While the amount of speech which can be stored is strictly limited at present, this restriction will be eased, bringing worthwhile speech output systems within the range of CALL enthusiasts using microcomputers. One part of the improvement is that storage is becoming cheaper. In addition, research is leading to ways of using significantly less storage space for a given length of speech. It is possible to compress the digital pattern to a tenth of the length previously required (for example, using the 'linear prediction method', Atal & Hanauer 1971). While storing less data about each sound leads to some loss of quality, the speech when played back is still up to studio tape-recording standard. Recent developments permit a further reduction in storage requirements and new possibilities for CALL, by allowing prosodic features to be stored and manipulated independently of the items with which they were associated in the original input (see the impressive work of Sanders and others in Suppes 1981:303–600). Work is also in progress on methods of synthesizing speech from phonemic code; the results are of great interest to the linguist but not as yet of adequate quality for language teaching (Sherwood 1981; McComb 1982).

To sum up our consideration of speech input/output, we may say that its usefulness in CALL is self-evident. At present, the quality of digitized speech already available is satisfactory and neither hardware nor software offers any great problem in its use. The major limitation is that the amount of speech which can be stored and output is small. However, we can hope for improvement in the near future. Once again, it is research into the nature of language itself which will take language teaching forward in this area.

8.5 Computer graphics and computer-based videodisc systems

Just as those engaged in CALL have wanted to add the spoken dimension to their work, they have also wanted to use pictures – whether still or moving. Hence attempts to link slide-projectors and video-recorders to computers. However, like tape-recorders, these are not ideal devices to partner a computer and their use has not caught on to any significant extent. There are two more promising ways of making pictures available. The first is to produce line drawings on the screen of the VDU or monitor; this is known as computer graphics and it has the advantage that the entire process occurs within the computer system. The second possibility is to use an external device which is fully compatible with computers – the videodisc. We discuss the two options in turn.

8.5.1 Computer graphics

The term **computer graphics** refers to the computer's ability to draw a line between two points on a screen under the control of a program. Superficially this seems to be simple enough. However, not all terminals can cope with this. Many VDUs can display only the characters on a normal typewriter or teletype keyboard. These characters, generated under the control of a computer system, can be displayed only from left to right to a maximum of eighty (sometimes 120) per line; the gap between the lines is also fixed.

Graphics programming requires that the screen should be controlled by a microprocessor, enabling the user to decide where to position the cursor. For this the program author must use a **graphics programming language**. The alternative is to write programs in a low-level language, which involves detailed instructions for the simplest of cursor movements. This work is extremely time-consuming and tedious. Graphics programming languages contain a simple set of commands like PENUP, PENDOWN, PLOT, MOVE, ERASE, BLINK, etc. For colour terminals the language may contain yet another command, COLOUR, and codes or commands to select the colour for the foreground (writing or drawing) and for the background. Most microcomputer systems have graphics programming languages with varying degrees of sophistication. This is an area where those using microcomputers often have an advantage over those using mainframes. There are also devices available (on some mainframes and on some microcomputers) which reduce programming to a minimum by enabling the program author to 'draw' directly into the computer. The **light pen** is a short rod attached to the terminal by a wire; the user draws on the screen and the computer displays the lines drawn and, at the same time, automatically records them in the form of digital data. An alternative pointing device is the so-called **mouse**. The mouse is usually connected to the computer by a wire. As the user moves the mouse on the desk, the cursor is moved on the VDU screen. Once the cursor is in position (say beside the desired item on a list or by a picture sign, known as an 'icon') the user presses a button on the mouse and an appropriate command is issued to the computer. This device will speed up the process of developing CALL materials, but it could also be used as an input device by the learner. Some computers provide a **graphics tablet**, which looks like a simple tray. The user places on it the picture or diagram which he or she wishes to reproduce and traces the outline with a special pen. Again, the computer copies the lines on to the screen and records them. Unfortunately, the different techniques involved make graphics one of the least portable of computer facilities.

An important use of graphics for CALL purposes is the drawing of character sets (alphabets) other than that found on the standard keyboard. If it is possible to draw lines, then one can draw other characters. Indeed, CALL programs exist for Russian, Hindi, Armenian and Chinese, among others. One method is patiently to write the software to draw each character (see Ahmad & Corbett 1981 for an example).

However, various character sets are now available (in software form) relatively cheaply for many microcomputers and it is much easier to buy them and make adjustments if required. It is also possible to have a new character generator EPROM (Erasable Programmable Read Only Memory) chip made commercially. If one is in the enviable position of buying a microcomputer solely for CALL purposes, then it is worth finding out whether there is a suitable microcomputer designed for the country of the target language, with all the required characters. Certain microcomputers are sold in different versions for the main West European languages.

Naturally, the capability to draw a line between two points means that simple pictures can be drawn. (The principle is as in join-the-dots pictures: the greater the number of dots and the shorter the lines, the more realistic the picture.) It is easy to see the value of having outline drawings under the control of the CALL program. One could, for example, display a simple map of the South of England, Belgium and Northern France, including the main towns and the cross-channel routes. This could form the basis for practice of prepositions: *John is IN Paris, he is going VIA Dieppe, he is going BY boat* and so on. A timetable could also be displayed, with questions as to when John will get home if he goes by a certain route – mastering timetables in the foreign language is a skill well worth acquiring.

From a static outline drawing one can progress to moving pictures. The program draws, for example, a picture of a boy by giving appropriate co-ordinates on the screen, and using the PLOT command to relate the co-ordinates to the left hand side of the screen. The next instruction is to ERASE the picture of the boy, change the co-ordinates so that the picture is displayed slightly to the right and PLOT the co-ordinates again. The picture is redrawn in less than a tenth of a second and to the student it appears that the boy has just moved to the right. The alternation of the ERASE and PLOT commands will create the illusion of the boy running across the screen. The program to move the boy across the screen, sail a ship or whatever, can be controlled by a more conventional CALL program, with explanation, questions and so on. In fact, the co-ordinates of various objects can be stored and called up when required by different programs. The potential applications are numerous. Spatial and motion expressions can be presented clearly, for example, the complexities of verbs of motion in Russian (where motion 'there and back' requires a different verb from that used for motion 'one way') or difficult combinations such as *out of, down from, up to,* and *along past* in English.

An attractive alternative, used in the PLATO system, is to offer a 'menu' of articles, nouns, prepositions and verbs. The student makes a selection: provided the result is a grammatical sentence the computer 'shows it' on the screen (even if semantically unlikely). Thus, if the choice is: *the tree jumps over the house,* a little house and tree appear on the screen and the tree indeed jumps over the house. This is an example of a common technique, particularly in programs for younger learners, namely the use of graphics as a reward for completing a linguistic task. This approach is particularly effective with a touch-sensitive screen: the young learner touches the words in order on the screen rather than having to type them in.

The graphics commands BLINK and COLOUR mentioned above also deserve comment. BLINK allows a selected portion of text, from a prefix to a paragraph, to be blinked on and off on the screen. It is excellent in restricted use, particularly in the presentation of new material, but vertiginous if overused. Sanders & Kenner (1983:37) suggest a good use of this facility in exercises based on running text which examine cohesive devices. The student is asked to indicate, say, what a pronoun such as *it* refers to in context, and this can be highlighted by making the antecedent blink on and off.

Colour too can be handled by many computers, provided that a colour monitor is attached. A domestic television can be used, but the quality may sometimes be disappointing. Colour can be used to structure sections of text or to enhance diagrams, as well as in pictures. Its use requires imagination and skill and the results can be striking. Colour can be controlled by writing software commands, while some computers allow the user to 'paint' using a light-pen. When one adds the possibility of using colour on the screen, whether as an integral part of the CALL program or merely to render the graphics element more attractive, then it is clear that the graphics capability is a powerful CALL tool. Graphics techniques can be mastered by a CALL teacher conversant with a simple programming language like BASIC. It is also important to note that some author languages like TUTOR have a graphics supplement. The trend is that these facilities are becoming easier to use and so they are likely to play an increasing role in CALL.

8.5.2 Computer-driven videodisc systems

While the use of computer graphics is ideal when an outline picture is sufficient (as it frequently is for language learning), there are circumstances when high-quality, realistic pictures are desired. Some teachers have worked with videotape, controlling the video-recorder by computer (for technical details see Hallgren 1980). There are interesting possibilities, but videotape, like audiotape, is a linear device and suffers from the same disadvantage – the relatively slow speed at which a particular section of the tape can be found and played. For this reason, the videodisc has a lot to commend it. It offers advantages in quality and convenience and it can be successfully partnered with computer systems.

Laser-based videodisc systems are video playback systems capable of reproducing TV pictures and stereo or two-channel sound from a pre-recorded disc. The audio-visual data are densely packed in a reflective spiral sealed inside a disc. Two such discs bonded back to back give a complete videodisc, playable on both sides. The data are read by laser light which is locked on to a track by a servo-controlled optical system which maintains exact focus and synchronization. Since there is no mechanical contact between the optical system and the videodisc there is minimum wear and tear. This ensures long life and reliability.

Videodisc systems can store 55,500 frames on each side of the disc, or thirty-seven minutes of continuous play on each side. Videodiscs are recorded with one frame of information on each revolution and the disc can be spun at 1500 revolutions per minute. On typical systems any of the 55,500 frames can be accessed in two or three seconds. This direct access to any part of the disc contrasts with the linear search necessary on a videotape. Some videodisc systems have a communications interface, which allows the video system to be operated under the control of an external computer system. The size of the computer system, or indeed its make, is not an important consideration as long as it has a communications interface compatible with the videodisc system's interface. (For technical details see Schneider & Bennion 1981.)

The external computer system can be programmed to display the frames in any order predetermined by the CALL teacher. The external system can also 'freeze' frames, display any frame again and, more importantly for a CALL environment, the computer system can invite the student to key in responses to various questions via the keyboard. Depending on the student's response, the computer system can output messages (the text appears on the same screen as the pictures) and indeed 'branch off' to other parts of the disc to ask further questions.

If the disc is used to store single images, then it takes the place of the slide-projector but with the immense advantage of being able to show any of its many thousand pictures in seconds (Otto 1983); this is particularly valuable for 'civilization-type' courses. For many purposes, moving pictures are more useful and, as mentioned above, the technology allows the same possibilities as film – and more. Imagine we have a short scene taking place in a London street. The clear pictures and stereo sound make the presentation extremely lifelike. It could be followed by a set of questions. On receiving an incorrect answer, the computer would instruct the videodisc system to display the relevant section of the film again (which it will display with an accuracy unknown to the video-cassette), with an option for the student to review it until the point has been grasped. As the different frames can be accessed accurately and in any order, the teacher can select useful extracts from an entire disc. This technique involves the teacher in selecting passages from a commercially produced videodisc, just as teachers have used commercial films in the past. Production of videodiscs specifically for CALL purposes has problems, mainly financial. Good-quality video material is very expensive to produce. The important factors are the production costs (as for videotape) and the post-production (or mastering) costs.

A striking example of what can be done, given extensive resources, is reported by Schneider & Bennion (1983), who have created a disc-based CALL package called 'Montevidisco' for students of Spanish. At the beginning of the session, the disc sets the scene in a Mexican village. Then a man leaning against a wall walks towards the camera and asks in Spanish, 'You're an American tourist, aren't you?' The student is offered a list of alternative responses on the adjacent computer screen. He or she selects one and is asked to say it. This response is recorded on a standard cassette-recorder and the student can then hear the response given by a native speaker, to check and correct pronunciation. The sequence in the village then continues. This technique is important in a number of respects: partly because of the way in which it integrates videodisc, cassette and standard CALL formats, but even more for the way in which it draws the student directly into dialogue in context, responding to real-life situations. Not all users of videodisc will be able to go to such lengths. There are, fortunately, cheaper alternatives for those of us whose resources are more limited, since a lot of language-teaching material is already available on film or video-cassette. Commercial vendors may in some cases be persuaded, at a cost, to waive the copyright protection on a video-cassette for a single educational establishment. Once such video-cassettes are available to a CALL teacher, he or she may edit the tape to add a new audio track, or intersperse it with new video material, stills, slides or artwork. This may lead to a new premaster video-cassette, which can be used to produce the videodisc, acquired much more cheaply than by starting from the beginning.

For the future, we may hope that the mastering costs will be reduced and that publishers will transfer materials previously available on video-cassette to videodiscs. For the present, the much cheaper alternative of using already available videodiscs is more attractive. Taking a longer view, the place of the videodisc seems assured. The clarity of the pictures (including single frames), the speed and convenience of access to any part of the disc and its durability make it a valuable part of a CALL system.

8.6 Conclusion

New options are opening up for CALL at a rapid rate. Significantly large sections of the foreign language can be stored and accessed, both as dictionary entries and as continuous text. Developments in linguistics and artificial intelligence suggest ways to make CALL programs more sophisticated and more receptive to the learner's needs. Technological developments hold out the prospect of adding the dimensions of sound and pictures to CALL. Thus language-learning resources will be supplemented in exciting and innovative ways.

Conclusion

This book has given a broadly based introduction to computers in language learning, planned around the needs of the teacher with little or no previous knowledge of CALL or computers. The reader should now know enough about the subject to approach the computer from a more informed viewpoint and with a critical perspective.

CALL is an educational medium with considerable potential. The essential hardware and software for serious applications of computers to language learning are already available (chapter 2), and the history of CALL, though relatively short, has already given rise to a substantial body of experience and positive results (chapter 3). The time is therefore ripe for productive co-operation between linguists, language teachers and the computer. Ideas on second-language acquisition are changing rapidly and CALL is sure to be affected (chapter 4).

The person just starting to work in CALL has a range of packages to examine, with a choice of acceptance, enhancement or rejection. Some criteria for evaluation were suggested in chapter 5. There are different ways of acquiring or producing such packages, depending on how deeply the teacher wishes to become involved in programming. A set of materials can be bought, or they may be borrowed and perhaps improved. The next step is the creation of new materials from scratch. As we saw in chapter 6, there are two main approaches. Using an author language is certainly the easier option, though it restricts the author somewhat. The alternative is to learn a programming language, which is not as difficult as is commonly supposed. This may well be of value to the language teacher not only for the scope it gives when developing CALL materials but also for the light it sheds on natural language. In chapter 7 we discussed how CALL can be integrated into the language-teaching curriculum. We examined possible extensions to the techniques and activities available to the language teacher, as well as the ways in which the computer is constrained as a medium for natural language. We also considered the evaluation of CALL. Developments in computing (hardware and software) and in linguistics and artificial intelligence offer new prospects for CALL (chapter 8). Particularly in computing, what is not possible now may well be soon, since change is occurring both rapidly and radically.

While so many areas of education are being restricted, computers are becoming cheaper, more powerful and more accessible, and funds are being made available to buy them. In this favourable situation, CALL is in great need of original thinkers: people who will take note of the advances as they occur and who will devise new types of material to take full advantage of the resources available. One way to keep abreast of these continuing developments is through journals and newsletters; here the 'Useful addresses' section provides a starting point. It is also very helpful to be in close contact with a group of colleagues working in the same area, in order to discuss new ideas and problems, and to exchange successful CALL materials.

From time to time teachers come into contact with theories, ideas and methods which prompt them to think afresh about their profession. Whether the language teacher chooses to create new CALL programs or simply to use ready-made ones, he or she will be forced to think about the nature not just of language learning but also of language itself.

Useful addresses

Associations and projects

ACAL, Association for Computer-Assisted Learning, Educational Computing Section, Chelsea College, University of London, Pulton Place, London SW6 5PR, UK

ADCIS, Association for the Development of Computer-Based Instructional Systems, Computer Center, Western Washington University, Billingham, WA 98225, USA

ALLC, Association for Literary and Linguistic Computing, Secretary: Dr T. N. Corns, Department of English, University College of North Wales, Bangor, Gwynedd LL57 2DG, UK

AUCBE, Advisory Unit for Computer-Based Education, Endymion Road, Hatfield, Hertfordshire AL10 8AU, UK

CEDAR, Computers in Education as a Resource, Imperial College of Science and Technology, London SW7 2AZ, UK (until Summer 1984)

CERL, Computer-Based Education Research Laboratory, University of Illinois, Urbana, IL 61801, USA (PLATO System)

CET, Council for Educational Technology for the United Kingdom, 3 Devonshire Street, London W1N 2BA, UK

CIC, Computers-in-the-Curriculum Project, Chelsea College, Hudson Buildings, 552 Kings Road, London SW10 0UA, UK

CILT, Centre for Information on Language Teaching and Research, Regent's College, Inner Circle, Regent's Park, London NW1 4NS, UK

E/MU Project, Secretary: Mr L. Burr, Horwood Language Centre, University of Melbourne, Parkville 3052, Victoria, Australia

GEM Project, c/o Gavin Bell, Teachers' Resources Centre, St Paul Street, Aberdeen AB1 1DA, Scotland

ITMA, Investigations in Teaching with Microcomputers as an Aid, College of St Mark and St John, Derriford Road, Plymouth PL6 8BH, UK

MAPE, Micros and Primary Education, St Helen's County Primary School, Bluntisham, Cambridgeshire, UK

MEP, Microelectronics Education Programme, Cheviot House, Coach Lane Campus, Newcastle-upon-Tyne NE7 7XA, UK

MUSE, Micro Users in Schools and Education, Freepost, Bromsgrove, Worcestershire BG1 7BR, UK

NATE, National Association for the Teaching of English, 49 Broomgrove Road, Sheffield S10 2NA, UK

ORDI, Université Paris VII, Tour centrale 8e étage, 2 Place Jussieu, Paris 75005, France

SMDP, Scottish Microelectronics Development Programme, Dowanhill, 74 Victoria Crescent Road, Glasgow G12 9JN, Scotland

TESOL CALL Interest Section, Chairman: David Sanders, CALL-IS, Language Lab, Concordia University, 1455 de Maisonneuve Blvd. West, Montreal, Quebec H36 1M8, Canada

Current bibliographies

Computer-Based Language Learning (available from CILT – address above)

Annotated Bibliography of Articles concerning Computers in Education available from: Professor V. Stevens, Hawaii Preparatory Academy, Box 428, Kamuela, Hawaii 96743, USA

Journals and newsletters

British Journal of Educational Technology, (Council for Educational Technology – see above)

CALICO, Computer Aided Language Learning and Instruction Consortium, 229 KMB, Brigham Young University, Provo, Utah 84602, USA

CALLBOARD, Treasurer: Roger Savage, 19 High Street, Eccleshall, Stafford ST21 6BW, UK

CALNEWS (CEDAR – see above)

CET News (Council for Educational Technology – see above)

Computer Education, The Computer Education Group, North Staffordshire Polytechnic, Blackheath Lane, Stafford ST18 0AD, UK

Computers in Schools (MUSE – see above)

Educational Computing, 30-31 Islington Green, London N1, UK

L'APOP, Le Bulletin de l'Association pour les Applications Pédagogiques de l'Ordinateur au Post-Secondaire, a/s Louise Lessard, Collège Bois-de-Boulogne, 10 555 av. Bois-de-Boulogne, Montreal, Canada

Journal of Computer-Based Instruction, Association for the Development of Computer-Based Instruction Systems, 3255 Hennepin Avenue South, Minneapolis, MN 55408, USA

MALL, Society for Microcomputer Applications in Language and Literature, University Station, Box 7134, Provo, UT 84602, USA

PIPELINE, P.O. Box 388, Iowa City, IA 52244, USA

Software publishing houses

Arnold-Wheaton Software, Parkside Lane, Dewsbury Road, Leeds LS11 5TD, UK

Cambridge Micro Software, Cambridge University Press, The Edinburgh Building, Shaftesbury Road, Cambridge CB2 2RU, UK

CAMSOFT, 10 Wheatfield Close, Maidenhead, Berkshire SL6 3PS, UK

Educational Software for Microcomputers, Duke Street, Wisbech, Cambridgeshire P13 2AE, UK

Gessler Publishing Co Inc., 900 Broadway, New York, NY 10003, USA

Heinemann Computers in Education Ltd, 22 Bedford Square, London WC1B 3HH, UK

Hutchinson Education, Hutchinson House, 17-21 Conway Street, London W1P 6JD, UK

Longman Microsoftware, Longman Group Resources Unit, 33-35 Tanner Row, York YO1 1JP, UK

MUSE Software Librarian, PO Box 43, Hull, UK

NELCAL, Freepost, Thomas Nelson and Sons Ltd., Nelson House, Walton-on-Thames, Surrey KT1 4BR, UK

Soft Centre, Renvyle Cottage, Okehurst Lane, Billingshurst, West Sussex RH14 9HR, UK

Wida Software, 2 Nicholas Gardens, London W5 5HY, UK

Further information from:

DOES, Directory of Educational Software (forthcoming), Triumph House, 189 Regent's Street, London W1, UK

Sources for machine-readable texts

International Computer Archive of Modern English, The Norwegian Computing Centre for the Humanities, P.O. Box 53, University of Bergen, 5014 Bergen, Norway

Oxford Archive, Oxford University Computing Service, 13 Banbury Road, Oxford OX2 6NN, UK

Bibliography

This bibliography contains only publications which are referred to in the book. For fuller listings of earlier work in CALL see Allen (1973a) and Birdsong (1977). A more up-to-date annotated bibliography is available from CILT and a fuller one from Vance Stevens (see 'Useful addresses' section). A resource bibliography specifically concerned with microcomputers has been compiled by Hertz (1983). For a comprehensive bibliography see Stevens, Sussex & Tuman (forthcoming).

Adams, E. N., Morrison, H. W. & Reddy, J. M. 1968. Conversation with a computer as a technique of language instruction. *Modern Language Journal*, 52, 1:3–16. (Reprinted in Atkinson & Wilson 1969)

Ahl, D. H. 1973. *101 Basic Computer Games*. Maynard, Mass., Digital Equipment Corporation

Ahmad, K., Colenso, M. & Corbett, G. 1978. On the teaching of Russian numerals by using an online computer. *Association for Literary and Linguistic Computing Bulletin*, 6, 3:235–41

Ahmad, K. & Corbett, G. G. 1981. Bilingual terminals: input and output in Cyrillic and Roman scripts. In Wildenberg (1981), pp. 237–52

Ahmad, K., Corbett, G. G. & Edwards, J. M. 1978. Developments in computer assisted learning for Russian. *Russian Language Journal*, 32, no. 113:37–42

Ahmad, K. & Rogers, M. 1979. GERAD: an adjective morphology teaching program. *Journal of Computer-Based Instruction*, 6, 2:55–9

1981. Development of teaching packages for undergraduate students of German. In Wildenberg (1981), pp. 253–63

Alford, M. 1971. *Computer Assistance in Learning to read Foreign Languages: An Account of the Work of The Scientific Language Project*. Cambridge, Literary and Linguistic Computing Centre

Allen, J. R. 1972. Current trends in computer-assisted instruction. *Computers and the Humanities*, 7, 1:47–55

1973a. A bibliography of computer-assisted instruction. *System*, 1, 2:30–53

1973b. The cybernetic centaur: advances in computer-assisted instruction. *Computers and the Humanities*, 7, 6:373–87

Aplin, T. R. W., Crawshaw, J. W., Roselman, E. A. & Williams, A. L. 1981. *Introduction to Language*. London, Hodder & Stoughton

Atal, B. S. & Hanauer, S. L. 1971. Speech analysis and synthesis by linear prediction of the speech wave. *Journal of the Acoustical Society of America 50*, 2:637–55

Atkinson, R. C. 1968. Computerised instruction and the learning process. *American Psychologist*, 23:225–39. (Reprinted in Atkinson & Wilson 1969)

Bibliography

Atkinson, R. C. & Wilson, H. A., editors, 1969. *Computer-Assisted Instruction: A Book of Readings.* New York, Academic Press

Austin, J. L. 1962. *How to Do Things With Words.* Oxford, Oxford University Press

Bar-Hillel, Y. 1960. The present status of automatic translation of languages. In *Advances in Computers: Volume I*, ed. F. L. Alt, A. D. Booth & R. E. Meagher, pp. 91–163. New York, Academic Press

Barker, P. G. & Singh, R. 1982. Author languages for computer-based learning. *British Journal of Educational Technology*, 13, 3:167–96

Barr, A. & Feigenbaum, E. A., editors, 1982. *The Handbook of Artificial Intelligence: Volume II*, London, Pitman

Bell, R. T. 1981. *An Introduction to Applied Linguistics: Approaches and Methods in Language Teaching.* London, Batsford Academic and Educational

Birdsong, D. 1977. *Computer-Assisted and Programmed Instruction in Foreign Languages: A Selected, Annotated Bibliography.* Arlington, VA, ERIC Clearinghouse on Languages and Linguistics. (CAL-ERIC/CLL series on languages and linguistics, 50)

Blomeyer, R. L. 1984. *Computer-Based Foreign Language Instruction in Illinois Schools: A Review of Literature, Some Preliminary Observations, and Recommendations.* Technical report number LLL-T-4-84. Urbana, University of Illinois at Urbana-Champaign, Language Learning Laboratory

Bott, M. F. 1970. Computational linguistics. In *New Horizons in Linguistics*, ed. J. Lyons, pp. 215–28. Harmondsworth, Penguin

Brown, H. D. 1973. Affective variables in second language acquisition. *Language Learning*, 23:231–44

Brumfit, C. 1984. *Communicative Methodology in Language Teaching: The roles of fluency and accuracy.* Cambridge, Cambridge University Press

Brumfit, C. J. & Johnson, K. 1979. *The Communicative Approach to Language Teaching.* Oxford, Oxford University Press

Bruner, J. S. 1966. Notes on a theory of instruction. In *Cognitive Development in the School Years*, ed. A. Floyd, 1979, pp. 273–83. London, Croom Helm in association with the Open University Press

Burke, R. 1983. *CAI with PILOT.* Englewood Cliffs, NJ, Prentice-Hall

Cerri, S. & Breuker, J. 1981. A rather intelligent language teacher. *Studies in Language Learning*, 3:182–92

Chandler, D., editor, 1983. *Exploring English with Microcomputers.* London, Council for Educational Technology in association with the National Association for the Teaching of English

Chapelle, C. & Jamieson, J. 1983. Language lessons on the PLATO IV system. *System*, 11, 1:13–20

Chomsky, C. 1969. *The Acquisition of Syntax in Children from 5 to 10.* Cambridge, Mass., MIT Press

Chomsky, N. 1959. Review of B. F. Skinner, *Verbal Behaviour.* In *Language*, 35:26–58

1976. *Reflections on Language*, Glasgow, Fontana/Collins

Clahsen, H. 1980. Psycholinguistic aspects of L2 acquisition: word order phenomena in foreign workers' interlanguage. In *Second Language Develop-*

ment (Trends and Issues), ed. S. W. Felix, pp. 57–79. Tübingen, Gunter Narr Verlag

Clark, W. H. & Clark, G. M. 1966. Achievement in elementary German under programmed and conventional instruction: a preliminary study. *Modern Language Journal*, 50:97–100

Coupland, J. 1983. Software – an historical overview. In Chandler (1983), pp. 99–107

Cromer, 1970. 'Children are nice to understand': surface structure clues for the discovery of a deep structure. *British Journal of Psychology*, 61, 3: 397–408

Curtin, C. Avner, A. & Provenzano, N. 1981. Computer-based analysis of individual learning characteristics. *Studies in Language Learning*, 3:201-13

Curtin, C. Clayton, D., Finch, C., Moor, D. & Woodruff, L. 1972. Teaching the translation of Russian by computer. *Modern Language Journal*, 56, 6:354-60

Curtin, C., Cooper, P. & Provenzano, N. 1981. Russian reading course. In *Higher Education PLATO Courseware*, pp. 218-27. Eagan, MN, Control Data Corporation

Curtin, C., Dawson, C. L., Provenzano, N. & Cooper, P. 1976. The PLATO system: using the computer to teach Russian. *Slavic and East European Journal*, 20, 3:280-92

Davies, G. 1980. Learning German by computer at Ealing College of Higher Education. *CALNEWS*, 15, September 1980:5-8

1982. *Computers, language and language learning*. With a section on the use of the computer in ELT by J. Higgins. (CILT information guide no. 22). London, Centre for Information on Language Teaching

Demaizière, F. 1983. Les questions que rencontre l'utilisateur de l'enseignement assisté par ordinateur (EAO), *Les langues modernes*, 77:11-26

Dodson, C. 1967. *Language Teaching and the Bilingual Method*. London, Pitman

1978. The independent evaluator's report. In *Bilingual Education in Wales 5-11*, report by E. Price, pp. 47-53. London, Evans Brothers and Methuen Educational for the Schools Council

Dulay, H., Burt, M. & Krashen, S. 1982. *Language Two*. New York, Oxford University Press

Edwards, J. M. 1981. *The implementation of a translation aid on a mini*. MTech thesis, Brunel University

Farrington, B. 1981. Computer based exercises for language learning at university level. In *Computer Assisted Learning: Selected Proceedings from the CAL 1981 Symposium held on 8-10 April 1981 at the University of Leeds*, ed. P. R. Smith, pp. 113-6. Oxford, Pergamon. Special issue of *Computers and Education* (volume 6, number 1, 1982)

Felix, S. W. 1982. *Psycholinguistische Aspekte des Zweitspracheneriverbs*. Tübingen, Gunter Narr Verlag

Fields, C. & Paris, J. 1981. Hardware-software. In *Computer-Based Instruction: A State-of-the-Art Assessment*, ed. H. F. O'Neil, pp. 65-90. New York, Academic Press

Bibliography

Goodyear, P. & Barnard, A. 1982. Microcomputers and special education: survey and prospects. In Smith (1982), pp. 61-73

Hallgren, R. C. 1980. Interactive control of a videocassette recorder with a personal computer. *Byte*, 5, no. 7:116-34

Harrison, C. 1983. English teaching and computer-assisted simulations. In Chandler (1983), pp. 83-8

Hart, R. S., editor, 1981a. *The PLATO system and language study*. Special issue of *Studies in Language Learning* (=volume 3, number 1). Urbana-Champaign, Language Learning Laboratory, University of Illinois

    1981b. Language study and the PLATO system. *Studies in Language Learning*, 3:1-24

Hartnett, R. T. 1974. Adult learners and new faculty roles. *Findings*, 1, 3:1-4

Hatch, E. 1974. Second language learning – universals. *Working Papers on Bilingualism*, Ontario Institute for Studies in Education, Toronto, Canada, 3:1–17

Hawkins, E. 1981. *Modern Languages in the Curriculum*. Cambridge, Cambridge University Press

Henisz-Dostert, B., MacDonald, R. R. & Zarechnak, M., editors, 1979. *Machine Translation*. The Hague, Mouton

Hertz, R. 1983. *Microcomputers in Bilingual and Foreign Language Instruction: A Guide and Bibliography*. Los Alamitos, National Centre for Bilingual Research

Higgins, J. 1982. How real is a computer simulation? *ELT Documents*, 113:102–9

    1983. Computer assisted language learning. *Language Teaching*, 16, 2:102–14

Higgins, J. & Johns, T. 1984. *Computers in Language Learning*. London, Collins ELT

Higman, B. 1967. *A Comparative Study of Programming Languages*. London, MacDonald

Hockey, S. & Marriott, I. 1980. *Oxford Concordance Program, Version 1.0, User's manual*. Oxford, Oxford University Computing Service

Hocking, E. 1970. Technology in foreign language teaching. *Modern Language Journal*, 54:79–91

Howard-Hill, T. H. 1979. *Literary Concordances: A Guide to the Preparation of Manual and Computer Concordances*. Oxford, Pergamon

Howe, J. A. M. & du Boulay, B. 1979. Microprocessor assisted learning: turning the clock back? *Programmed Learning and Educational Technology*, 16:240–6. (Reprinted in Rushby 1981)

Jenkins, C. 1980. *Language Links: The European Family of Languages*. London, Harrap

Jensen, K. & Wirth, N. 1978. *PASCAL User Manual and Report* (second corrected reprint of the second edition). New York, Springer-Verlag

Johns, T. F. 1981. The uses of an analytic generator: the computer as teacher of English for specific purposes. *ELT Documents*, 112:96–105.

    1983. Generating alternatives. In Chandler (1983), pp. 89–97

Johnson, K. 1982. *Communicative Syllabus Design and Methodology*. Oxford, Pergamon

Karriker, R. J. 1976. *Beginning Bulgarian: A Programmed Language Course*, Ph.D. dissertation, Stanford University

Kenning, M-M. & Kenning, M. 1981. Computer assisted language teaching made easy, *British Journal of Language Teaching*, 19, 3:119–23, 136

Kenning, M. J. & Kenning, M. M. 1982. EXTOL: an approach to computer-assisted language teaching. *Association for Literary and Linguistic Computing Bulletin*, 10, 1:8–18.

   1983. *An Introduction to Computer Assisted Language Teaching*. Oxford, Oxford University Press

King, M. 1982. Eurotra: an attempt to achieve multilingual MT. In Lawson (1982), pp. 139–47

Knowles, F. E. 1982. The Russian language and the computer. In *Papers in Slavonic Linguistics: I*, ed. F. E. Knowles & J. I. Press, pp. 93–110. Birmingham, University of Aston, Department of Modern Languages

Krashen, S. D. 1977. The Monitor Model for adult second language performance. In *Viewpoints on English as a Second Language*, eds. M. Burt, H. Dulay & M. Finocchiaro, pp. 152–61. New York, Regents Publishing Co.

   1978. Individual variation in the use of the Monitor. In *Principles of Second Language Learning*, ed. W. Ritchie, pp. 175–83. New York, Academic Press

   1981. *Second Language Acquisition and Second Language Learning*. Oxford, Pergamon Press

Krutch, J. 1981. *Experiments in Artificial Intelligence for Small Computers*. Indianapolis, Howard W. Sams

Kulik, J. A., Kulik, C.-L. & Cohen, P. A. 1979. A meta-analysis of outcome studies of Keller's personalized system of instruction. *American Psychologist*, 34:307–18

Kulik, J. A., Kulik, C.-L. & Cohen, P. A. 1980. Effectiveness of computer-based college teaching: a meta-analysis of findings. *Review of Educational Research*, 50, 4:525–44

Last, R. W. forthcoming a. *Language Teaching and the Micro*. Oxford, Blackwell

   forthcoming b. Teaching your computer to talk. To appear in *Modern Languages in Scotland*

Lawson, V., editor, 1982. *Practical Experience of Machine Translation: Proceedings of a Conference: London, 5–6 November 1981*. Amsterdam, North-Holland

Lehnert, W. G. & Ringle, M. D., editors, 1982. *Strategies for Natural Language Processing*. Hillsdale, NJ, Erlbaum

Littlewood, W. T. 1974a. Programmed instruction and language teaching. *Modern Languages*, 55:12–16

   1974b. Communicative competence and grammatical accuracy in foreign language learning. *Educational Review*, 27, 1:34–44

   1981. *Communicative Language Teaching*. Cambridge, Cambridge University Press

Lumsdaine, A. A. & Glaser, R., editors, 1960. *Teaching Machines and Programmed Learning: A Source Book*. Washington, Department of Audio Visual Instruction, National Education Association of the United States

McComb, G. 1982. Speech, speech! *Creative Computing* 8, 12:120–3

Bibliography

MacDonald, R. R. 1979. The problem of machine translation. In Henisz-Dostert, MacDonald & Zarechnak (1979), pp. 89–145

McEwen, N. 1977. Computer-assisted instruction in second-language learning: an Alberta project. *Canadian Modern Language Review*, 33:333–43

McGettrick, A. D. 1980. *The Definition of Programming Languages*. Cambridge, Cambridge University Press

Markosian, L. Z. & Ager, T. A. 1983. Applications of parsing theory to computer-assisted instruction. *System*, 11:65–77

Meyer, S. R. 1960. Report on the initial test of a junior high school vocabulary program. In Lumsdaine & Glaser (1960), pp. 229–46

Morrison, H. W. & Adams E. N. 1968. Pilot study of a CAI laboratory in German. *Modern Language Journal*, 52:279–87. (Reprinted in Atkinson & Wilson 1969)

Moto-oka, T. *et al.* (unspecified) 1982. Challenge for knowledge information processing systems. In *Fifth Generation Computer Systems: Proceedings of the International Conference on Fifth Generation Computer Systems: Tokyo, Japan, October 19–22, 1981*. ed. T. Moto-oka, pp. 1–89. Amsterdam, North-Holland

Mueller, T. H. 1968. Programmed language instruction – help for the linguistically "underprivileged". *Modern Language Journal*, 52:79–84

1972. The development of curricular materials (including programmed material) for individualized foreign language instruction. In *Individualizing Foreign Language Instruction: The Proceedings of the Stanford Conference*, eds. H. B. Altman & R. L. Politzer, pp. 148–64. Rowley, Mass., Newbury House

Mueller, T. H. & Niedzielski, H. 1966. Programmed instruction in teacher retraining (NDEA institutes). *Modern Language Journal*, 50:92–7

Munby, J. 1978. *Communicative Syllabus Design*. Cambridge, Cambridge University Press

Nash, A. & Ball, D. 1982. *An Introduction to Microcomputers in Teaching*. London, Hutchinson

Olmsted, H. M. 1975. Two models of computer-based drill: teaching Russian with APL. *Slavic and East European Journal*, 19, 1:11–29

Olsen, S. 1980. Foreign language departments and computer-assisted instruction: a survey. *Modern Language Journal*, 64, 3:341–9

Ornstein, J. 1968. Programmed instruction and educational technology in the language field: boon or failure? *Modern Language Journal*, 52:401–10

O'Shea, T. & Self, J. 1983. *Learning and Teaching with Computers: Artificial Intelligence in Education*. Brighton, Harvester Press

Otto, S. K. 1983. Videodisc image retrieval for language teaching. *System*, 11:47–52

Papert, S. 1980. *Mindstorms: Children, Computers, and Powerful Ideas*. Brighton, Harvester Press

Porter, D. 1960. A report on instructional devices in foreign language teaching. In Lumsdaine & Glaser (1960) pp. 186–205

Prince, M. M. & Casey J. P. 1972. Programmed instruction helps teach Spanish grammar. *Modern Language Journal*, 56:491–2

Pusack, J. P. 1983. Answer-processing and error correction in foreign language CAI. *System*, 11:53–64

Ramer, A. 1976. Syntactic styles in emerging language. *Journal of Child Language*, 3:49–62

Roberts, A. H. 1973. Current problems in computer-assisted language instruction. *Rassegna Italiana di Linguistica Applicata*, 5, 1:19–40

Roberts, G. W. 1983. Reviews of computer assisted language learning programs. *The British Journal of Language Teaching*, 21, 1:62–8

Rogers, M. A. 1984. On major types of written error in advanced students of German. *International Review of Applied Linguistics*, 22:1–39

Rosenbaum, P. S. 1968. The computer as a learning environment for foreign language instruction. *IBM Research Report RC–2352*. (Reprinted in *Foreign Language Annals*, 2, 1969, 4:457–65)

Rushby, N., editor, 1981. *Selected Readings in Computer-Based Learning*. London, Kogan Page

Sanders, D. & Kenner, R. 1983. Whither CAI? The need for communicative courseware. *System*, 11:33–9

Schank, R. C. 1979. Natural language, philosophy and artificial intelligence. In *Philosophical Perspectives in Artificial Intelligence*, ed. M. Ringle, pp. 196–224. Brighton, Harvester Press

Scherr, B. P. & Robinson, L. W. 1980. Creating computer-assisted drills for Russian: the structure of the database. *Russian Language Journal*, 34, no. 118:21–36

Schneider, E. W. & Bennion, J. L. 1981. *Videodiscs*. Englewood Cliffs, NJ, Educational Technology Publications.

1983. Veni, vidi, vici via videodisc: a simulator for instructional conversations. *System*, 11:41–6

Schupbach, R. 1973. *Toward a Computer-Based Course in the History of the Russian Literary Language*. Technical report 221. Stanford, Stanford University, Institute for Mathematical Studies in the Social Sciences. (Published version as 'Computer-assisted instruction for a course in the history of the Russian literary language' in Suppes 1981, pp. 657–64)

Searle, J. R. 1969. *Speech Acts: An Essay in the Philosophy of Language*. London, Cambridge University Press

Sharples, M. 1981a. A computer written language lab. *Computer Education*, 37:10–12.

1981b. A computer-based teaching scheme for creative writing. In *Computers in Education: Proceedings of the IFIP TC-3, 3rd World Conference on Computers in Education – WCCE 81, Lausanne, Switzerland, July 27–31, 1981* ed. B. Lewis & D. Tagg, pp. 483–8. Amsterdam, North-Holland

1983. A construction kit for language. In Chandler (1983), pp. 51–8

Sherwood, B. 1981. Speech synthesis applied to language teaching. *Studies in Language Learning*, 3: 171–80

Sinclair, J. M. & Coulthard, R. M. 1975. *Towards an Analysis of Discourse: The English used by Teachers and Pupils*. London, Oxford University Press

Skinner, B. F. 1954. The science of learning and the art of teaching. *Harvard Educational Review*, 24:86–97. (Reprinted in Lumsdaine & Glaser 1960)

Bibliography

Slagle, J. R. 1971. *Artificial Intelligence: The Heuristic Programming Approach.* New York, McGraw Hill

Smith, I. C. H., editor, 1982. *Microcomputers in Education.* Chichester, Ellis Horwood

Starkweather, J. A. 1969. A common language for a variety of conversational programming needs. In Atkinson & Wilson (1969), pp. 269–304

Stevens, V., Sussex, R. & Tuman, W. forthcoming. *A Bibliography of Computer-Aided Language Learning*

Stewart, J. 1983. Does the use of the microcomputer inhibit the development of language in children? In Chandler (1983), pp. 59–74

Suppes, P., editor, 1981. *University-Level Computer-Assisted Instruction at Stanford: 1968–1980.* Stanford, Stanford University, Institute for Mathematical Studies in the Social Sciences

Suppes, P. & Morningstar, M. 1969. Computer-assisted instruction. *Science,* 166, 343–50

Sussex, R. 1983. CALL: the computer as a tool for language learning. *Australian Review of Applied Linguistics,* 6, 2:53–9

Taylor, B. 1975. The use of overgeneralisation and transfer learning strategies by elementary and intermediate students in E.S.L. *Language Learning,* 25:73–107

Taylor, H. F. 1979. Students' reactions to computer assisted instruction in German. *Foreign Language Annals,* 12, 4:289–91

Van Campen, J. A. 1968. *Project for Application of Mathematical Learning Theory to Second-Language Acquisition, with Particular Reference to Russian.* Final Report. Stanford University, California Community College Planning Centre. Report to US Office of Education, Contract No. OEC-0-8-001209-1806. (Published version as 'A computer-assisted course in Russian' in Suppes 1981, pp. 603–46)

1973. *A Computer-Based Introduction to the Morphology of Old Church Slavonic.* Technical report 205. Stanford, Stanford University, Institute for Mathematical Studies in the Social Sciences. (Published version as 'A computer-assisted introduction to the morphology of Old Church Slavic' in Suppes 1981, pp. 665–74)

Van Campen, J., Markosian, L. Z. & Seropian, H. 1980. *A Computer-Based Language Instruction System with Initial Application to Armenian.* Technical report 303. Stanford, Stanford University, Institute of Mathematical Studies in the Social Sciences. (Published version as 'A computer-assisted language instruction system with initial application to Armenian' in Suppes 1981, pp. 717–33)

Van Ek, J. A. & Alexander, L. G. 1980. *Threshold Level English.* Oxford, Pergamon

Waite, S. V. F. 1970. Computer-supplemented Latin instruction at Dartmouth College. *Computers and the Humanities,* 4, 5:313–4

Weaver, W. 1949. *Translation.* New York, mimeograph

Weizenbaum, J. 1976. *Computer Power and Human Reason: From Judgement to Calculation.* San Francisco, W. H. Freeman

Whitelock, P. J. 1983. Machine translation. *AISB Quarterly: Newsletter of the*

Society for the Study of Artificial Intelligence and Simulation of Behaviour, 48:18–20

Widdowson, H. G. 1978. *Teaching Language as Communication.* Oxford, Oxford University Press

Wildenberg, D., editor, 1981. *Computer Simulation in University Teaching.* Amsterdam, North Holland Publishing Company

Wilkes, S. J. C. 1979. C.A.L. in language teaching at King Edward VI Five Ways School. *Computer Education,* 33:7–11

Wilkins, D. A. 1974. *Second-Language Learning and Teaching.* London, Edward Arnold

1976. *Notional Syllabuses.* Oxford, Oxford University Press

Winograd, T. 1972. *Understanding Natural Language.* Edinburgh, Edinburgh University Press

1973. A procedural model of language understanding. In *Computer Models of Thought and Language.* Eds. R.C. Schank & K. M. Colby, pp. 152–86. San Francisco, W.H. Freeman

1983. *Language as a Cognitive Process: Volume I: Syntax.* Reading, Mass., Addison Wesley

Wisbey, R. A. 1962. Concordance making by electronic computer: some experiences with the 'Wiener Genesis'. *Modern Language Review,* 57, 2:161–72

Wyatt, D. H. 1983a. *Computer-assisted learning in ESL.* Washington, DC, Center for Applied Linguistics

editor, 1983b. *Computer-Assisted Language Instruction* Special issue of *System* (=volume 11, number 1). Oxford, Pergamon Press

Zarechnak, B. 1979. The history of machine translation. In Henisz-Dostert, MacDonald & Zarechnak (1979), pp. 1–87

Index